Praise for
EASY. WHOLE. VEGAN.

"*Easy. Whole. Vegan.* offers a fantastic variety of healthy and easy-to-make recipes that both vegans and non-vegans will love. You'll want to bookmark every page!"
—KATIE HIGGINS, author and founder of *Chocolate-Covered Katie*

"First she did it with nut milks and nut butters. Now, vegan genius Melissa King once again proves how easy it is to kick processed foods to the curb. *Easy. Whole. Vegan.* serves up no-fuss meals, snacks, and treats for the entire family!"
—IVY LARSON, author of *Clean Cuisine*

"Melissa King has again created simple, affordable, and original whole-food recipes that make the transition from the SAD diet to whole foods, easy and exciting. From indulgent and nostalgic Creamy Mushroom Risotto and Chocolate Espresso Pudding to refreshing dishes like Energizing Green Juice, Strawberry Salsa, and Creamy Orange Pops, *Easy. Whole. Vegan.* is a wonderful resource for a variety of plant-based recipes. This collection takes the intimidation and complication out of healthy cooking and highlights seasonal produce and other nutrient-packed foods!"
—ASHLEY COX, vegan chef and creator of thenakedfoodlife.com

Praise for
DIY NUT MILKS, NUT BUTTERS & MORE

"If you're ready to move beyond store-bought boxes of almond milk and jars of natural peanut butter, King's small book is the perfect guide to homemade nutty goodness."
—PORTLAND PRESS HERALD

"When I tested [the Chocolate Almond Banana Cups] in the Bauer house this past weekend everyone FLIPPED OUT! Best part? There's only 5 ingredients and the recipe's super-simple to whip together."
—JOY BAUER, *Today* show host and founder of Joy Bauer Nutrition

"*DIY Nut Milks, Nut Butters & More* is an essential resource for anyone who wants to eat well, go homemade, and make the most of an amazing ingredient. Strawberry brazil nut milk, cinnamon pecan butter, almond joy cookies (!)—I could go on and on. Whether you're just beginning to make more homemade staples or you've been making nut milk for years and want to take it to the next level, Melissa King has you covered."
—ALANA CHERNILA, author of *The Homemade Pantry* and creator of eatingfromthegroundup.com

"Melissa's delicious staples and treats make healthy living so accessible. You'll never buy commercial products again, when you see how easy it is to create pure, natural food with just a few ingredients. I will be giving this book to every mother I know."
—TESS MASTERS, author of *The Blender Girl*

ALSO BY MELISSA KING

DIY Nut Milks, Nut Butters & More

EASY.
WHOLE.
VEGAN.

EASY.
WHOLE.
VEGAN.

100 FLAVOR-PACKED, NO-STRESS RECIPES *for Busy Families*

Melissa King

THE EXPERIMENT

NEW YORK

Easy. Whole. Vegan.: *100 Flavor-Packed, No-Stress Recipes for Busy Families*
Copyright © 2016 by Melissa King
Photographs © 2016 by The Experiment

The Experiment, LLC
220 East 23rd Street, Suite 301
New York, NY 10010-4674
www.theexperimentpublishing.com

This book contains the opinions and ideas of its author. It is intended to provide helpful and informative material on the subjects addressed in the book. It is sold with the understanding that the author and publisher are not engaged in rendering medical, health, or any other kind of personal professional services in the book. The author and publisher specifically disclaim all responsibility for any liability, loss, or risk—personal or otherwise—that is incurred as a consequence, directly or indirectly, of the use and application of any of the contents of this book.

Many of the designations used by manufacturers and sellers to distinguish their products are claimed as trademarks. Where those designations appear in this book and The Experiment was aware of a trademark claim, the designations have been capitalized.

The Experiment's books are available at special discounts when purchased in bulk for premiums and sales promotions as well as for fundraising or educational use. For details, contact us at info@theexperimentpublishing.com.

Library of Congress Cataloging-in-Publication Data

Names: King, Melissa (Melissa G.), author.
Title: Easy, whole, vegan : 100 flavor-packed, no-stress recipes for busy
  families / Melissa King.
Description: New York, NY : Experiment, LLC, [2016]
Identifiers: LCCN 2016011258 (print) | LCCN 2016023792 (ebook) | ISBN
  9781615193097 (pbk.) | ISBN 9781615193103 (ebook)
Subjects: LCSH: Vegan cooking. | Quick and easy cooking. | LCGFT: Cookbooks.
Classification: LCC TX837 .K4975 2016 (print) | LCC TX837 (ebook) | DDC
  641.5/636--dc23
LC record available at https://lccn.loc.gov/2016011258

ISBN 978-1-61519-309-7
Ebook 978-1-61519-310-3

Cover and text design by Sarah Smith
Photographs by Heather Poire
Author photograph on page 212 by Marcus King

Manufactured in China
Distributed by Workman Publishing Company, Inc.
Distributed simultaneously in Canada by Thomas Allen & Son Ltd.

First printing August 2016
10 9 8 7 6 5 4 3 2 1

This book is dedicated to my husband, Marcus.
Thank you for the countless hours you spent helping me with this book.

Contents

EASY: EFFORTLESS SLOW COOKER DISHES

MAKE AHEAD: REFRIGERATOR-FRIENDLY MEALS

ENTERTAIN: FAVORITES FOR A CROWD

MAKE IT YUMMY: SAUCES, DRESSINGS & OTHER ACCOMPANIMENTS

PICK-ME-UPS: JUICES & SMOOTHIES

Introduction

Our Story

It's amazing how seemingly unrelated events, small suggestions, and giant leaps of faith can bring you to a point in your life you never would have imagined. I've been a vegetarian for the past sixteen years, but it wasn't until I made the decision to become vegan and gluten-free that I realized how many processed foods I was consuming—far from whole food and worlds away from plant-based. The decision to follow a vegan, gluten-free, and whole food diet really started with my children, my two little girls who make my husband and me feel like the luckiest people alive.

In September 2009 we had our first daughter, Meadow. It was a difficult journey from the get-go. After a pregnancy riddled with complications, Meadow was born with multiple gastrointestinal issues, including a milk-protein allergy, acid reflux, and delayed gastric emptying. It was heartrending to see her vomit and refuse food to the point of dehydration on an almost daily basis. Knowing what to feed her was a struggle and a constant point of stress for the whole family.

In May 2011, while living in Las Vegas, we had our second daughter, Olive, after another difficult pregnancy. Olive is my miracle baby. Born with restricted growth (meaning she was much smaller than she should have been), she was quickly diagnosed with a milk-protein allergy, acid reflux, malabsorption, and "failure to thrive." With no local family support and few friends willing to help us, we decided it was time to move back to our home state of Texas, where we could get the support we desperately needed. We packed up and started our trek to Dallas—across the desert— that summer. In hindsight, a four-day road trip through triple-digit temperatures with two sick babies in the backseat was probably not the best idea. Before we made it to Dallas,

Olive stopped eating. In desperation, Marcus put Olive and me on a plane to fly the rest of the way.

Marcus drove with Meadow and met us late in the afternoon the same day. It wasn't looking good at that point. Olive was definitely getting dehydrated, and the next morning we took her to a nearby hospital. We expected her to get some IV fluids and be sent on our way. We had done this with Meadow so many times before in Las Vegas. The hospital staff weighed her, asked us some basic questions, and put us in a room. This is where things started to take a different turn. The ER doctor walked in, took a look at the chart, then glanced at Olive and told us she was preparing a room for our daughter in the pediatric unit. She was being admitted. The doctor said any nine-week-old child who only weighs nine pounds and who has stopped eating needed to be admitted. This seems so obvious now, but at the time we were shocked. Funny how that works. That ER trip turned into a thirteen-day hospital stay crammed full of all varieties of tests. While there, Olive was diagnosed with dysphasia, an affliction that caused her to inhale formula into her lungs instead of swallowing it into her stomach. In essence, she was drowning every time she ate.

She left with a feeding tube, and we were instructed to give her continuous feedings through the tube with medical-grade formula. We were told the NG (nasogastric) tube—a small tube placed through one nostril, down the throat, and into the stomach—would provide necessary nutrients and reduce vomiting. One week later, though, she was still vomiting. The doctors readmitted her to the hospital and implanted a G-tube (gastronomy tube), a small port that protruded from her belly and went directly into her stomach. Another part of that surgery was supposed to make it nearly impossible for her to vomit. While the surgery did allow us to easily feed her, she still vomited constantly.

It was unbearable to watch Olive struggle. Financially, we were in a bad place, too. Medical-grade formula tends to be very expensive. However, several months later, when Olive was fourteen months old, our lives were transformed. Her feeding therapist had a seemingly small suggestion that would alter things forever: Start a blended diet of real foods for her instead of using medical-grade formula. We loved the idea, and luckily her doctors were on board as well. This led our entire family down a whole food path and was the first step on an even longer journey that led to my blog, my first cookbook, and now *Easy. Whole. Vegan.* While researching what to feed Olive, a nutritionist told us to be sure to buy organic food. She said pesticide residue in conventional produce could cause more harm than good. We had never heard anything like that before. Since we had to be careful what we fed her, we started researching the ingredients in our foods. We were shocked at what we found. It appeared that processed foods marketed as "healthy" were actually the opposite. The "low-fat diet" was nothing more than a marketing ploy. These were a series of eye-opening moments for us.

When Olive started her whole food, plant-based, blended diet, the vomiting ceased altogether—pretty much overnight. A sparkle came into her eyes and her personality began to shine more than ever before. Meadow, then three years old, also took to eating fresh fruits and raw vegetables. She became an active participant in the kitchen, helping us prepare the food. Her health began to turn around, too. Amazed at the turnaround in both our daughters, my husband and I started making changes in our own diet.

In my twenties and early thirties I would never have imagined or believed I'd become a cookbook author and food blogger. Before I started down this path, my idea of cooking was warming up store-bought veggie burgers. I had a huge sweet tooth, and I could never quite shake those five pounds I was looking to lose despite eating all the low-fat foods that marketers said were good for me.

After I started eating a whole food, plant-based diet, largely absent of processed foods, I began to notice changes. My sweet tooth seemed to subside almost overnight, and those five pounds I couldn't lose turned into ten pounds lost. My husband, who suffered from chronic allergies and asthma his whole life, no longer needed any of his medications. His doctor was amazed at the reversal of his cholesterol numbers. We were no longer burdened by past ailments as we began our new adventure.

More importantly, my daughters have benefited the most from our whole food diet. We value the process of nourishing their bodies with healthy food, having gone through our past struggles. We want to include them in our healthy meals, introduce them to new foods, and provide them with the many vitamins and nutrients their growing bodies need. Your whole family, too, can benefit from eating these plant-based, gluten-free, whole food meals—with this book, deciding what to feed your family for every meal becomes so much simpler.

Easy, Whole, Vegan Meals for Busy Families

Being healthy in today's society is not an easy task. With restaurants on every corner serving up some kind of comfort food, it's no surprise we struggle with health issues such as heart disease, obesity, and diabetes. Since it's all too easy to revert to an unhealthy lifestyle, we have to find a way that makes healthy eating not only quick, but efficient, too. Things are easier when they can be done quickly and without complications. We all live busy lives, and if our time spent in the kitchen isn't fun, we resort to ordering pizza for the night. The easy, simple recipes in this book show that being healthy only requires you to spend a little bit of time in the kitchen to get great results. A lot of people think they don't have time to be healthy or they have to give up their favorite foods, but that simply isn't true. Being healthy to me is about eating plant-based, whole foods wrapped up as delicious dishes that I can whip up at any time.

The recipes in this book are organized in such a way that takes all the guesswork out of cooking—by need rather than meal type. I've included here recipes for breakfasts and brunches, soups and salads, sides and appetizers, entrées, snacks, desserts, smoothies, and more. Looking for a meal you can prepare in thirty minutes or less? I've got you covered. How about an effortless dish you can come home to? My easy slow cooker dishes are the answer! Everyone talks about meal planning, but some dishes keep better than others. My make-ahead recipes are refrigerator-friendly—I even provide information on how long they'll last if stored. You'll also never wonder what to make for

a crowd again. Even better, I've provided recipes for all kinds of sauces, dressings, and other accompaniments to make your meals extra-yummy! Recipes like Coconut Whipped Cream, vegetable broth, and Basic Cashew Cream are used in other recipes and will become staples in your whole food pantry as well. And finally, pick-me-ups in the form of smoothies and juices are sure to keep your family going.

My husband and I have been living a whole food lifestyle for quite some time now. We've been able to stay on track because we've found ways to make effortless, healthy meals for the whole family. We don't want to spend hours tending to a boiling pot with fifty ingredients, or have to prep complex marinades the night before. Many of my recipes have short ingredients lists for that very reason and require minimal prep time. We want good flavor and hearty meals that require no fuss. We strive to use just a few ingredients and common spices that most people already have around the house to whip up something that everyone can enjoy. We don't want to spend an hour after a meal cleaning up pots, pans, and every utensil in the kitchen. Our cooking system works for us, and it should work for you, too.

If you're an on-the-go type of person who wants great tasting food but is sick and tired of being sick and tired, try these quick and easy meals to live a whole food, plant-based life. By taking the obstacles of not enough time and too much complexity out of your way, you'll find the whole food life is one you not only want to live, but will want to share with family and friends as well.

The Whole Food Vegan Pantry

A t a glance, my pantry looks similar to any other pantry, filled with grains, flours, sugars, spices, and much more. The main difference between my kitchen and others is my use of whole foods over processed foods. My recipes include fresh fruit, vegetables, herbs, spices, and other all-natural ingredients. This is what whole foods mean to me. I use the freshest ingredients and shy away from processed foods. The vegan and gluten-free goods in my recipes can be found at your local grocery store, health food store, or farmers' market. I choose organic and unprocessed options whenever possible. The ingredients that follow are things I keep in my kitchen and use in this book.

APPLESAUCE

I often use applesauce in place of oil in baking recipes. Whenever I call for applesauce, it will always be unsweetened. If you can't find unsweetened applesauce, you can make your own by blending up an apple in a food processor or high-power blender (see Homemade Applesauce, page 92, for a full recipe). If you have an allergy to apples, you can often use pumpkin purée instead. Applesauce also makes a great healthy snack for young children.

ARROWROOT POWDER

Arrowroot powder acts as a wonderful thickener—I often use it to thicken soups and sauces. Since many people avoid corn products (or have corn allergies), arrowroot is a great replacement for cornstarch. It's derived from a variety of tropical plants native to Central and South America and is completely gluten-free.

BAKING POWDER AND BAKING SODA

Baking powder and baking soda are both leavening agents—they cause baked goods to rise. Baking soda is also used to help neutralize the acids in a recipe and contributes to the texture as well. When looking for baking powder, make sure you choose a brand that's aluminum-free. Baking soda doesn't contain aluminum, so you can buy any brand you like. It's important to note that baking powder has a shelf life of about twelve months. Once it's expired, it will not cause baked goods to rise. One way to test your baking powder to see if it's still good is to put 1 teaspoon in ½ cup (120 ml) of boiling water. If it bubbles, it's still good. If you're out of baking powder, you can make your own by combining ¼ cup (40 g) of cream of tartar with 2 teaspoons of baking soda. Baking soda, on the other hand, has a very long shelf life; it can last up to three years.

BRAGG LIQUID AMINOS

Bragg Liquid Aminos is a great gluten-free alternative to soy sauce. It has a very similar taste to soy sauce without the added fillers, is made from non-GMO soybeans and purified water, and is not fermented. Like soy sauce, it can also add great flavor to stir-fries and sauces. Use coconut aminos as a soy-free alternative.

CHIA SEEDS

These little seeds pack a nutritional punch. They're a great source of fiber *and* protein. When hydrated, they become sticky and help things congeal. You can make pudding (see the Blueberries & Cream Chia Pudding, page 95) or energy drinks with them, and I like to add them to baked goods, granola, overnight oats (see Salted Caramel Overnight Oats, page 136), or raw treats. They're quite versatile, so if you plan on doing some whole food baking, it's a good idea to keep these around.

CHICKPEA FLOUR

I discovered chickpea flour about a year before I started writing this book. It's naturally gluten-free and very easy to work with. I use it mostly to make my chickpea omelets (Tomato Basil Chickpea Omelets, page 30), but it can also be used to make pancakes and baked goods. It has a very distinct texture that's different from typical flours. If you can't find chickpea flour at the store, you can make your own using a high-power blender. Just grind up dried chickpeas into flour. Please do not attempt to make this in anything other than a high-power blender such as a Vitamix or Blendtec.

CHOCOLATE

Just because you eat whole foods doesn't mean you can't have chocolate—it can be part of a whole food pantry when used in moderation. As a general rule of thumb, I only use dark chocolate (65 percent cacao or greater), as most dark chocolate is dairy-free. I buy the Endangered Species brand of chocolate bars since they're fair trade and vegan. Chocolate chips can also be used in moderation; I like to use Enjoy Life chips, which are dairy-free, gluten-free, and nut-free. They do contain a small amount of sugar, so I suggest using them sparingly.

Cacao powder is the raw form of chocolate, made by cold-pressing cacao beans, which keeps all the nutrients. It's very bitter in flavor. Cocoa powder is raw cacao that has been roasted at high temperatures, so it does not contain all the nutrients, but roasting does remove some of the bitter flavor. Cacao and cocoa are interchangeable in recipes.

COCONUT SUGAR

Despite the name, coconut sugar tastes nothing like coconut. It has a similar flavor to brown sugar or raw sugar, although its sweetness is much milder. Some people prefer coconut sugar as a sweetener because it has a lower glycemic index. That means it won't spike your blood sugar and then cause you to crash as so many processed sugars do. While I mostly use pure maple syrup in my recipes, I do use coconut sugar on occasion. It's a great option for when a recipe calls for granulated sugar. You can also make it the consistency of powdered sugar by grinding it up in a small blender or food processor.

COOKING OILS

I often use oils to sauté, roast, and stir-fry. Some oils that I keep on hand for cooking are coconut oil, avocado oil, and almond oil. Toasted sesame oil works well in stir-fries because of its rich flavor. I use olive oil and hemp oil for flavoring things. Avocado oil and olive oil are both great for salad dressings and cold dishes. I try to minimize my family's oil intake, though, so we use it only sparingly. If you don't use oil, that's fine; you can use vegetable broth or water for roasting or instead of sautéing.

DAIRY-FREE MILKS

These days there are many great dairy-free milk options. My milk of choice is almond milk. Where I call for almond milk in the book, I always use unsweetened. Other dairy-free milk options are hemp, oat, flaxseed, and quinoa. Although it's widely available in grocery stores, almond milk is very easy to make at home. Simply take 1 cup (140 g) of raw almonds and soak them in water overnight in a covered jar. Then rinse and drain the almonds and add them to a blender with 3 to 4 cups (720 to 960 ml) of fresh water. Blend until the consistency is smooth, then strain the liquid through a cheesecloth or nut milk bag. Make sure to squeeze all the moisture out. Essentially, you're milking the nuts. The liquid you squeeze out becomes the nut milk. The pulp left in the cheesecloth can be dried in the oven and used in gluten-free baking. This process works for all nuts, although some nut milks, such as pistachio or cashew, require no straining. For those, simply blend and serve. Homemade nut milk will keep in the fridge for about four days.

When it comes to adding rich, creamy flavors to recipes, I like to use full-fat canned coconut milk. You can find it in the international section of grocery stores. Coconut milk is also great for making dairy-free whipped cream.

DRIED BEANS

One of the things I noticed after switching to dried beans was how much cleaner they tasted than canned beans. It was pretty

BEAN TYPE	SOAKING TIME	COOKING TIME	PRESSURE COOKING
Black beans	4 hours	45 minutes to 1 hour	15 to 20 minutes
Garbanzo beans (chickpeas)	10 to 12 hours	1½ to 2 hours	20 minutes
Kidney beans	10 to 12 hours	1½ to 2 hours	20 to 25 minutes
White beans	10 to 12 hours	1½ to 2 hours	20 to 25 minutes
Pinto beans	10 to 12 hours	1½ to 2 hours	20 minutes

mind-blowing! Sure, they take a little longer to prepare, but once you get the hang of it, it's no big deal. Not only do they taste fresher, but they're much cheaper, too. I keep my dried beans stored in glass mason jars in my pantry.

When using dried beans, measure half the amount of cooked beans the recipe calls for, since they double in size after they've soaked. For example, for a recipe that calls for 2 cups (345 g) of cooked beans, you will need to measure out about 1 cup (190 g) of dried beans for soaking. Soak in a sealed container overnight. In the morning, boil the beans until soft. If you've never tried cooking with dried beans, I encourage you to give it a go. The handy table on page 9 gives you soaking/cooking times for dried beans.

Since not everyone uses dried beans, the recipes indicate the amount of canned beans needed. If you're using canned beans, always drain and rinse before adding them to the recipe.

DRIED FRUITS

I keep a lot of different dried fruits in my pantry. They're great for adding natural sweetness to oatmeal dishes (Oatmeal Snack Bars, page 123), cookies (Three-Ingredient No-Bake Almond Butter Cookies, page 166), granola (Carrot Cake Granola, page 96), chia pudding (Blueberries & Cream Chia Pudding, page 95), or even salads (Broccoli Salad, page 114). When I buy dried fruits, I look for the kind with no added sugars, with the exception of tart fruits such as cranberries or cherries, and then I look for the kind that has been sweetened only with fruit juice. Dried fruit also makes a great snack to satisfy a sweet tooth without having a lot of sugar.

EGG SUBSTITUTES

Just because you are vegan does not mean you need to avoid recipes that call for eggs. Egg replacers help bind, thicken, and set sauces, baked goods, and traditionally egg-containing dishes. It's very easy to substitute using any of the methods below. I use flax eggs for all of the recipes in this book, but all of these work well.

EXTRACTS

I use several different extracts in my baking. They add great flavor profiles to baked recipes. My favorites are vanilla, almond,

SUBSTITUTE	INGREDIENTS	PREPARATION
Flax egg	1 tablespoon flaxseed meal	3 tablespoons warm water; Whisk together and place in the fridge for 1 minute to thicken
Chia egg	1 tablespoon chia seeds, ¼ cup water	Whisk together and place in the fridge for 1 minute to thicken
Packaged egg replacer	1½ teaspoons Ener-G Egg Replacer, 2 tablespoons water	Stir together and let sit for 1 minute to thicken

and coffee extracts. The vanilla and almond extracts do contain alcohol, so I only recommend them for cooked recipes. The coffee extract I use is alcohol-free, so it can be used in raw recipes as well as cooked. If you have difficulty locating coffee extract in stores, you can buy it online at a pretty reasonable price. In a pinch, 1 teaspoon of ground instant coffee granules can be used in place of 1 teaspoon of coffee extract.

FLAXSEED MEAL

Flaxseed meal is just ground-up flaxseeds, which is a great source of protein, fiber, iron, and omega-3 fatty acids. It's better to consume flaxseed meal than whole flaxseeds; the body can more easily absorb the meal, whereas the seeds are hard to break down and fully digest. However, flaxseeds stay fresh longer than flaxseed meal, so I like to buy the seeds and then grind them up into a meal using a coffee grinder. I use flaxseed meal when making vegan egg replacements, known as a flax egg (see page 10 for instructions). You can also add flaxseed meal to smoothies and overnight oats to make them extra-nutritious.

GROUND VANILLA BEANS

Indigenous to Central and South America, vanilla has the amazing ability to make foods seem sweeter than they actually are. Because of this, I really love to use ground vanilla beans in my recipes. They help you keep the sugar content low and the flavor profile high. This is why just a little bit of vanilla goes a long way in any recipe. One of my favorite uses of ground vanilla beans is in no-bake dishes such as chia pudding, overnight oats, and raw desserts. You can use vanilla extract in place of the vanilla beans, but you may taste the alcohol in recipes that aren't cooked, so be cautious when substituting.

HEMP HEARTS

Hemp hearts, which are simply shelled hemp seeds, contain some powerful nutrition. High in omega-3 and omega-6 fatty acids, just 2 tablespoons of hemp hearts contain about 10 grams of protein. Besides their nutritional benefits, they're quite tasty, too, imparting a nice nutty flavor. You can throw them into oatmeal, smoothies, raw treats, and baked goods. You can even make milk with hemp hearts. Just blend 1 cup (150 g) of hemp hearts with 2 cups (480 ml) of water for a minute or two, until the consistency is smooth. Pour and serve. No straining necessary! Hemp hearts really are a must-have superfood for your kitchen. You can generally find them in the bulk bins or raw food aisles at most health food stores.

HERBS & SPICES

Herbs and spices are essential to the whole food vegan pantry. Some of the ones I like to use most include basil, cayenne, cinnamon, chili powder, cloves, cumin, garlic, ginger, mint, nutmeg, oregano, parsley, red pepper flakes, sage, smoked paprika, and turmeric. To save money, I buy my spices in bulk. Another great place to get spices is a Middle Eastern market, a trick I picked up from my Turkish mother-in-law. Spices are usually much less expensive there than at the grocery store.

Herbs are better when they're fresh, rather than dried (although it's good to keep some dried herbs on hand, just in case). The best way to store fresh herbs is to cut off the ends and place the herbs in a glass vase or jar filled with water. I suggest using different vases for each type of herb instead of throwing them all in the same one. It not only looks pretty, but it makes the herbs last for weeks!

LENTILS

Lentils are a great source of protein and an inexpensive alternative to other plant-based protein sources such as soy, beans, and nuts. They're also an excellent source of fiber, magnesium, and folate. Lentils come in many varieties, but the ones I use most often are red, green, and brown. I like red lentils best—they cook quickly and are slightly sweet. Green and brown lentils are larger, take a little longer to cook, and have more of an earthy taste. Lentils cook in the same way as rice, so you don't have to soak them ahead of time like you do for dried beans.

MEDJOOL DATES

I really can't say enough good things about this little fruit. I like the Medjool dates best because they're the largest and also the softest variety—they're a staple in my house. Although you can use another kind of date in my recipes, be aware that you may need to add a few more than the recipe calls for if your dates are smaller. Dates make the perfect paste for baking and provide a caramel-like consistency in raw desserts. I highly recommend stuffing one with almond butter for a sweet treat. If you don't want to use Medjool dates, you can always use figs or apricots in their place.

MIRIN

Even if you've never heard of mirin, you've probably tasted it before in Asian cooking.

Like sake, mirin is a rice wine. They differ, though, as mirin has a high sugar content and a very low alcohol content. It can be found in Asian markets, most health food stores, and the international sections of grocery stores. Mirin is often paired with soy sauce to offset its saltiness. If you can't find mirin, you can dissolve 1/2 teaspoon of coconut sugar into 2 tablespoons of white wine. Just mix together and add it in place of the mirin.

NUTRITIONAL YEAST

Nutritional yeast is nothing like bread yeast, so don't let the name deter you. As the name implies, though, it really is very nutritious. It's naturally gluten-free and high in B vitamins. B vitamins are not easily found in a plant-based diet, so this is a great natural source for them. Nutritional yeast has a cheesy, nutty flavor, so it's the perfect ingredient for making vegan nut cheeses (Macadamia Nut Cheese Sauce, page 171), and it's also quite delicious on popcorn (Cheesy Garlic Popcorn, page 51).

NUTS & NUT BUTTERS

Nuts are a great source of healthy fats and proteins, and for that I just love them. I eat homemade almond butter every single day. Nut butters are very versatile and work in both sweet and savory recipes. I often use them as a binder in raw desserts and even veggie burgers. If you have a nut allergy, you can usually use sunflower seeds or sunflower butter in recipes that call for nuts or nut butters. To make nut butter, just grind up the nuts in the food processor or blender. Some nuts take longer than others. Peanut, macadamia nut, and Brazil nut butter can be made in about 5 minutes. Other nut butters, such as almond or cashew, can take up to 20 minutes in the food processor or blender.

OAT FLOUR

Gluten-free oat flour is my flour of choice in baking. It's made from whole grains, and its texture is much lighter than whole wheat. I make my own oat flour by grinding up rolled oats in my food processor or high-power blender. You can also buy oat flour at the store. As with oats, it's important to look for oat flour that is certified gluten-free. If you have a sensitivity to oat products, you can use gluten-free all-purpose flour in place of oat flour in my recipes. Bob's Red Mill makes a gluten-free baking blend that can be used at a 1:1 ratio.

OATS

Oats come in several forms: oat groats (or oat berries), steel-cut oats, rolled oats, and quick-cooking (instant) oats. Oat groats refer to the whole, hull-less oat and are what you get when the inedible husk of the oat grain is removed. They're very hard and need to be soaked before using. Steel-cut oats are simply sliced oat groats. I like to use steel-cut oats in my overnight oats recipes (Salted Caramel Overnight Oats, page 136) because they retain a slight crunch. Rolled oats are oats that have been husked and then flattened. Quick-cooking oats are rolled oats that have been chopped into fine pieces to cook faster. Oats are naturally gluten-free, but they are often processed on the same machines as wheat, so if you have celiac disease or a sensitivity to gluten, look for certified gluten-free oats.

ONIONS

I use onions in a lot of my cooking, as do most people in America. Onions come in a wide variety, and each type can provide great flavor to any savory dish. Every kind of onion has different characteristics and can be used in many ways.

Thin green chives make a great garnish, and we tend not to cook them. Green onions, also known as scallions, look like long green tubes with white bulbs of varying sizes. The bulb is great to cook with and imparts a light onion flavor. The green stalk goes well in raw dishes. Like a chive, they are very mild. A shallot is a small, oblong, bulbous onion with a mild, sweet flavor. It's recognized by its red or copper skin and often contains two cloves inside. Shallots can be used raw or in cooking. White or yellow onions are much stronger in flavor and are typically used only in cooked dishes. They become sweet when cooked, but the onion flavor is still very apparent. These are our go-to onions in most savory dishes. The red onion is another onion we like to use. Its unique flavor makes it great both cooked and uncooked.

An uncooked onion will always have a much stronger flavor than its cooked counterpart. You'll notice that when one of my recipes uses raw red onion, I call for them to be sliced very thin or diced very small, almost minced. This cuts down on the pungent onion flavor, since it's thoroughly mixed in with the other ingredients.

PINK HIMALAYAN SALT

Have you ever tried pink Himalayan salt? You would think salt is just salt, but it comes in so many varieties these days, it's easy to get confused and flustered when trying to pick the right one for your dish. Since salt is an essential ingredient, it helps to get the best kind. Table salt and other processed, refined salts are stripped of their trace elements and minerals, resulting in a purer product. However, this makes it sticky, so salt manufacturers add anticaking agents to make it pour more easily from a salt shaker. Sea salt can contain trace amounts of heavy metals depending on how it's harvested. Pink Himalayan salt is mined, and it's pink because it contains a bit of iron oxide (i.e., rust). It helps balance our electrolytes and pH levels, improves circulation, and strengthens bones. Its larger crystals are also a bit easier to handle when sprinkling over food. I use it in all of my recipes that call for salt. You can find it at any health food store. If you prefer, you can use regular sea salt instead.

PRODUCE

Produce is a major part of the whole food vegan pantry. It's best to buy fruits and vegetables in their freshest state. Frozen is OK in a pinch, but fresh is ideal. To save money (and be more environmentally conscious), you should stick to buying produce that's in season—and local, if possible. Joining a CSA (Community Supported Agriculture) in your area is a great way to get fresh, local produce.

Do not store fruits and veggies together. Some fruits give off ethylene gas, which causes other produce to ripen more quickly. I have separate refrigerator drawers for my fruits and veggies. Produce that ripens or keeps better away from light in a cool, dry place can be stored in the pantry. Here is a list of the best places to store specific produce.

Refrigerator:

Apples	Cabbage	Eggplant
Bell peppers	Carrots	Leafy greens
Broccoli	Cucumbers	Squash & zucchini

Pantry:

Avocados	Onions	Tomatoes
Garlic	Potatoes	

Counter:

Oranges	Pears	Plums

MAPLE SYRUP

I like to use pure maple syrup as the primary sweetener in my baked goods, since it's more natural than refined sugars. I don't recommend using imitation pancake syrup. Plus there are some added benefits to using pure maple syrup. Since it's plant-based, it contains a high amount of polyphenols, which are known antioxidants. It's also less likely to cause issues such as indigestion or gas, compared to refined sugar. Although I personally don't use honey because it isn't vegan, if you prefer, you can use raw honey in place of pure maple syrup in any of my recipes—just substitute at an equal ratio.

QUINOA

Quinoa is a wonderful superfood. A great source of fiber and protein, it's actually one of the only plant-based complete proteins. It comes in seed form or in flakes. The seeds cook just like rice and can be used in place of rice in most dishes. The flakes are very similar to quick-cooking oats. I like to use quinoa flakes to add protein to smoothies and snack bars. Some people complain that quinoa has a bitter taste. To avoid this, you just need to give it a good rinse before cooking. Here are the steps for cooking perfect, fluffy quinoa.

1 Measure out 1 cup (170 g) of quinoa and pour it into a fine-mesh strainer.

2 Rinse the quinoa well with cold water. As you run the water over the quinoa, gently massage it with your hands. Do this for about 2 minutes.

3 Add the quinoa to a saucepan with 2 cups (480 ml) of water.

4 Bring it to a boil, turn the heat down to low, and simmer until all the water is absorbed, 15 to 20 minutes.

5 Once the quinoa is done, let it stand for 5 minutes.

6 Fluff the quinoa with a fork and serve.

RICE

Since rice contains traces of arsenic, I only cook with it on occasion. When I do, I like to use brown, black, or wild rice, the last being my favorite—it has a wonderfully nutty and earthy taste that does very well with earthy vegetables such as mushrooms. Before cooking, make sure you give your rice a good rinse in a fine-mesh strainer. Cook the rice with water or vegetable broth. It cooks best on the stove, using one part rice to two parts water (three for wild rice). Cook until the rice has softened. If there's still water left, place the rice in a fine-mesh strainer to drain the excess water. You can also use a rice

cooker and simply follow the manufacturer's instructions. If you don't serve the rice immediately after cooking, make sure to keep it covered, since it can dry out quickly. When you reheat rice, it's a good idea to add a teaspoon or so of water and cover as it reheats.

ROASTED RED PEPPERS

You can purchase roasted red peppers in a jar from the store if a recipe calls for them. However, making your own is not nearly as difficult as you might think. Just cut bell peppers in half, remove the seeds, and brush lightly with some oil. Then place them on a baking sheet and roast them in the oven at 350°F (180°C) for 45 to 60 minutes. Once they come out of the oven, let them cool off until they're OK to handle and remove the skins. If you're not using them immediately, store them in water in the refrigerator. If they're exposed to air, they tend to mold easily, but when stored in water they should keep for two to three weeks.

ROASTED TOMATOES

You can purchase an assortment of roasted tomatoes from the grocery store, or you can make them at home. They pack a lot of flavor and are very useful in cooking. It can take a little time to roast tomatoes, but you can do it when you have some free time and store them for later. Brush the tomatoes lightly in oil and bake them for 45 to 60 minutes at 350°F (180°C). Put the roasted tomatoes in an ice bath for 5 minutes. Once they're cool, remove them from their ice bath, peel the skins off, and roughly chop the tomatoes. Put the chopped tomatoes and their liquid in a jar and store it in the refrigerator. They'll keep for two to three weeks when sealed.

TAHINI

Tahini is a paste made from sesame seeds. It contains more protein than a lot of nuts, is full of calcium, and has a high fat content. It's used in hummus (Cucumber Dill Hummus, page 57) and can also be used to make fantastic dressings (Healthy Coleslaw, page 143). You can usually find it in the same section of the grocery store as nut butters, although sometimes it's in the international section. If you can't find it, you can use sunflower seed butter in its place, since it's similar in flavor.

TOFU & TEMPEH

You won't see a lot of recipes here that call for soy products, but I do occasionally eat fermented soy products like tempeh and soy sauce, and I also enjoy tofu. The dangers that many people associate with soy come from consuming a large amount of processed soy. If you stick to a plant-based, whole food diet, it's perfectly fine to enjoy soy products in moderation. I always make sure to buy soy products that are certified organic and non-GMO, since 90 percent of the soy in the US is genetically modified.

Tofu can be used in sweet or savory recipes, as it soaks up any flavors you add to it. It's important to note that tofu should be pressed before using, since it holds a lot of moisture. To press tofu, after you open the package, drain the water and then wrap the tofu in a paper towel. Gently press the tofu between your palms. This will release the excess moisture and allow the tofu to absorb the new flavors you add to it.

I like to bake mine ahead of time so I have it on hand to add to any dishes that call for it. To bake tofu, preheat the oven to 350°F (180°C). Cut the tofu in 1-inch (2.5 cm) cubes and place them on a baking sheet. Bake for about 35 minutes. Baked tofu should last about two weeks in the fridge.

Tempeh has a very earthy flavor, and I actually prefer it to tofu. I love to add tempeh to stir-fries (Veggie-Loaded Stir-Fry, page 119). It's great marinated in barbecue sauce as well.

VEGETABLE BROTH

Vegetable broth can be bought at the store, but making your own is very easy. All you need is the vegetable scraps you would normally throw away. Just save any odds and ends from prepping vegetables, such as carrot peels, celery trimmings, and onion ends. I keep mine in a bag in the freezer. Once the bag is full, I make vegetable broth. To make the broth, fill a large pot with water and dump in the vegetable scraps. Make sure the water is at least 4 inches (10 cm) above the veggies; it will reduce down as it cooks. Cover and cook on high for at least 6 hours. Once the broth is done, you can purée it with an immersion blender, or you can strain the solids out. I freeze my broth in serving-size containers, so I only have to defrost what I need.

Kitchen Equipment

There are many tools that will make your whole food life much easier. You'll find that some of them are already a part of your kitchen. If your budget is limited, the one kitchen appliance that I suggest you invest in is a good food processor. I built up my kitchen slowly over time. Don't fret or try to buy everything at once. You'll discover what tools you need as you experiment in the kitchen. In addition to the main cooking necessities, such as pots and bowls, I have listed some gadgets and tools to have on hand, such as a spiralizer, Microplane grater, and parchment paper. These tools are meant to make your time in the kitchen less about the mechanics and more about how rewarding cooking can be.

CITRUS PRESS

Lemons and limes are so versatile. They work well in sweet and savory recipes. I use both in many of the recipes in this book, so a good citrus press is essential. You can easily extract juice without having to worry about picking out seeds or getting your hands too dirty. If you want to go a little simpler, you can invest in a lemon reamer instead. We use both frequently.

CUTTING BOARD

While a cutting board is a given for most people, there are so many options out there it can make choosing a good one difficult. I have a set of bamboo cutting boards that I love. I find they have a longer life span than the plastic ones, which seem to fall apart pretty quickly. We hand-wash and hand-dry our cutting boards to keep them from getting too damaged. We also have to oil them on occasion with coconut oil to keep them from drying out and cracking. While the maintenance seems a bit high, they have lasted a really long time and still look brand-new.

DEHYDRATOR

Making my own fruit leathers is something I do often. It's so much cheaper to make your own, and there's no added sugar. I also create my own fun recipes, such as Cinnamon Banana Chips (page 125). In addition, dehydrators can make crackers (Sun-Dried Tomato Herb Crackers, page 156) or kale chips (Sriracha & Lime Kale Chips, page 54). Unlike the oven, the dehydrator will not heat up your kitchen, and you can run it even when you're not at home. I have an Excalibur 5-tray dehydrator. It is a little pricey, so if you have a smaller budget, I suggest going with a Nesco dehydrator. There are loads of reviews online to help you make the best decision for you and your family.

FINE-MESH STRAINER OR SIEVE

A fine-mesh strainer (or sieve) is a versatile gadget to have around. I use mine to drain dried beans after they're done soaking and for rinsing rice or quinoa. It's also useful for draining the water when cooking pasta or boiling veggies—this is especially helpful for one-pot dishes.

FOOD PROCESSOR

My food processor is the single most utilized appliance in my kitchen. It comes with several attachments that are very easy to use. It can finely chop veggies, blend nut butters and dips, and make dough for cookies and bars. I use a 7-cup (1.7 L) Cuisinart food processor. I find the size is just right for my needs, and it has been very reliable.

GLASS MIXING BOWLS

I use glass mixing bowls for making salads and mixing up granola bars or muffins. They also come in handy when you need to store something in the refrigerator and all your containers with lids are currently in use. They're simple to clean and don't stain, unlike plastic storage. I have a set of five different sizes.

GLASS STORAGE JARS

I'm trying to move away from using plastic products, so I have various sizes of mason jars for storage. I use the smaller jars for storing dressings, overnight oats, nut butters, and spices. The wide mouths on most glass jars work well for storing spices because I can get my measuring spoons inside them without a problem. I like to use the larger mason jars for storing soups and smoothies. We even use them to store cereals and crackers for our kids.

HIGH-POWER BLENDER

A high-power blender, such as a Blendtec or Vitamix, is very useful in a whole food kitchen—it blends up smoothies, sauces, and vegetables seamlessly. This is wonderful when you have picky little ones and want to hide veggies in your recipes. While a high-performance blender can set you back quite a bit, I recommend saving for one if you plan on becoming proficient in the kitchen. It was one of the first gadgets we saved to buy and is one of our most prized kitchen tools.

ICE CREAM MAKER

Some people may think an ice cream maker is a splurge, but it pays for itself pretty quickly. Have you bought organic ice cream lately? Even when you can find a good price, it often contains unwanted ingredients. The best thing about homemade ice cream is that you can control the ingredients and the amount of sugar that go into it. It also allows you to make your favorite ice creams without having to leave the house. If you think you can swing it, it's well worth the price.

ICE CREAM TUBS

After you make homemade ice cream (Blackberry Ice Cream, page 65), you'll need some place to store it. I like using the long Tovolo ice cream tubs. You can find them online or in home goods or kitchen supply stores. They're inexpensive and do a great job of storing the ice cream without freezer burn.

ICE POP MOLDS

In my house, ice pops are vessels for hiding vegetables. Blueberries help mask the color of greens, and mangoes and pineapples add enough sweetness to hide any veggie taste.

You can make any of the juice or smoothie recipes (pages 185 to 202) into ice pops by pouring them into molds and freezing. It's important to look for a brand that's BPA-free; I like Tovolo. To remove the ice pops from the mold, simply run the mold under hot water for a few seconds to loosen them enough to remove.

IMMERSION BLENDER

I love my immersion blender. It makes blending hot soups a snap. I used to have to transfer the hot liquid from the pot to the blender, but with an immersion blender, you just stick it in the pot and blend. Be careful, though—you can splash yourself quite easily.

JUICER

Some of the recipes in this book call for a juicer. Juicing is a great way to get a lot of vitamins in quickly, while giving your digestive system a break. I have a Breville juicer that is easy to use and clean. If you don't have a juicer and would like to make the juice recipes in this book, you can use a blender and then strain the liquid through a fine-mesh strainer.

MANDOLINE

A mandoline is great when you want to slice vegetables in a uniform size and shape (as in my Simple Cucumber & Dill Salad, page 112). They're pretty inexpensive, and you can find them in any kitchen supply store. Please use them with caution, because it can be easy to cut yourself . . . I learned the hard way.

MEASURING CUPS & SPOONS

Measuring cups and spoons are an essential part of any kitchen. I have a stainless-steel set that I love. It's held up much better than any of the plastic ones I owned in the past—the engraved measurements never wear off.

MICROPLANE

If you're like me and hate chopping garlic, then I highly recommend getting a Microplane grater—it minces garlic so quickly. It can also be used for zesting citrus, grating ginger and fresh turmeric, and much more. It's one of those gadgets you end up using more than you realize. It's worth the purchase and usually affordable.

PARCHMENT PAPER OR SILICONE BAKING MAT

Parchment paper for lining your baking sheets and pans eliminates the need for greasing. I personally use a nonslip baking mat like a Silpat on my baking sheets, but parchment paper works just as well. When I bake bars in a pan, I use parchment paper and leave a little hanging out the sides; that way I can easily lift out whatever I make.

POTS & PANS

The two pots I use the most are my large stockpot and my large sauté pan. I have a set of Cuisinart stainless-steel pots and pans that are still like new after ten years of use. I recommend buying stainless-steel pans rather than nonstick. Over time, nonstick surfaces can begin to decompose and flake off, and recent studies have indicated that the chemicals used to make pots and pans nonstick may be toxic, especially when used at high temperatures. While stainless-steel sets do cost more up front, you'll probably never have to buy another set, saving you money in the long run.

PREP KNIFE

A good set of knives, and more importantly a good prep knife, is key in any kitchen. A sharp, high-quality knife will save you tons of time in the kitchen, making any prep just breeze by. You'll also feel more confident as you go to cut up vegetables, since you won't have to slow down like you would for a dull knife. A serrated knife is good to have, too. It makes slicing tomatoes and other soft vegetables much easier.

ROLLING PIN

I use my rolling pin for making homemade crackers (page 156), especially when I need to roll the dough out super-thin. While I don't use it very often, it's nice to have around just in case.

SILICONE MUFFIN LINERS

Silicone muffin liners are an excellent addition to your kitchen. You can use paper liners, but if a recipe doesn't call for oil, the finished product will probably stick to the paper liners. The other issue with paper liners is the waste. They're one use and done. Silicone liners are easily cleaned, and food doesn't stick to them, making those oil-free recipes a breeze to bake. I recommend buying standard and jumbo sizes at the least. If you like smaller muffins, they make mini ones, too. They also come in a variety of colors.

SILICONE SPATULAS

If you're making sauces, or anything in a bowl for that matter, silicone spatulas allow you to get every last drop out of the bowl. You'll be amazed at how clean the bowl looks after you empty the ingredients out of it using a silicone spatula. They're also super-easy to clean and won't melt under high heat like plastic spatulas tend to do.

SLOW COOKER

I can't say enough good things about my slow cooker. It makes cooking in a pinch much easier. I actually have two slow cookers so I can cook two different things at once. You can make a lot more than stew in a slow cooker. In addition to savory dishes, I've made oatmeal, granola bars, and brownies, too. Some people even make slow cooker bread. It's a multipurpose appliance, right up there with my food processor. If you have a chaotic schedule and are always on the run, a slow cooker is a go-to item. Prep, set, walk away, and several hours later you have a large meal that will last for days.

SPIRALIZER

Spiralizers make vegetable noodles and so much more. There are several different kinds of spiralizers: an inexpensive handheld kind that can only do soft vegetables like cucumbers and zucchini and a countertop kind that can handle harder vegetables like sweet potatoes and beets. Sweet potato pasta is a must-try once you get a hold of one of these gadgets. They're amazing! Besides marveling at how useful it is, you'll feel like a kid again, having fun spiralizing all your vegetables.

STAND MIXER

Sure, you can mix most things by hand, but a mixer makes things much easier. I highly recommend a stand mixer. You can also use a handheld mixer, but be prepared for an arm workout! The stand mixer does an exceptional job making all sorts of things, including Coconut Whipped Cream (page 181)! It's also great for mixing together veggie burger ingredients. And, let's be honest, they're kind of a showpiece for your kitchen. Different brands are always on sale at one store or another, so keep an eye out and pick one up when you find it at the right price.

Tips to Save Time & Money

In today's world we all seem to lead pretty busy lives. Whether you're married, have kids, or are trying to further yourself in your career (or any combination of those!), time seems to get away from us all. And money? Who hasn't thought how nice it would be to have a bit more? Time and money management generally comes down to being organized. These tips and tricks can benefit you in two ways. They'll help you get in and out of the grocery store without spending more than you need, and will hopefully lower the grocery bill a bit over time as you learn how to shop on a whole food, plant-based diet. Next, they will teach you how to enjoy cooking without feeling like you spend all your time in the kitchen. Following a whole food, plant-based lifestyle doesn't mean you have to give up the life you've worked hard to obtain.

1. Buy in bulk. Buying grains, dried beans, and nuts from bulk bins is often cheaper than buying prepackaged brands. Try stocking up when you're able to catch these items on sale. Some other things I buy in bulk are salt and spices. This saves a good amount of money in an area that can quickly get pricey.

2. Plan meals. Meal planning is key to saving time and money. Figure out your meals for the week, make a grocery list according to those meals, and then head to the store. This will allow you to stick to your food budget and not buy unnecessary items at the store. You won't come home with a bunch of duplicate items that you already have at home and then have to watch something go bad because you can't use it in time.

3. Batch cook. Cooking in batches is essential for my family. On the weekends, I often have the stove, oven, and slow cooker all going at the same time. Because we already planned our meals for the week and have all the ingredients on hand (see previous tip), we're able to lessen our time in the kitchen. When we're done cooking, I store each dish in serving-size containers so they can be pulled out quickly for an easy meal. This also makes it easy for my husband to take lunch to work.

4. Love your slow cooker and freezer. This goes along with the previous tip. Stocking your freezer with premade meals keeps you from stressing out if you have a hectic day creep up on you or you have a busy weekend in store and you know you won't be able to cook. Stressing about cooking is a surefire way to slip up, stop eating healthy, and instead find convenience in non-homemade, processed foods.

5. Buy seasonal produce. Buying produce in season often leads to a cheaper grocery bill. Our grocery stores are full of produce from around the world, so we're rarely aware of what's in season and what isn't, but those items that aren't in season are higher in price. It's done so slowly you don't recognize that the cost is going up. Join a CSA (Community Supported Agriculture) in your area for added savings, as they cut out the middleman and bring food directly from the farmers. You can buy extra produce when it's in season and freeze it to use the rest of the year. To freeze most fruits and veggies, you can just lay them flat on a baking sheet lined with parchment paper and place it in the freezer. Once the produce is frozen, pop it into freezer bags to store. It's important to label everything you put into the freezer, not only with the name of the items, but also with the date that the items were placed in the freezer.

6. Prep raw veggies and hummus for snacking during the week. I like to cut up enough peppers, celery, and carrots for an entire week. If I get an urge to snack during the week, I can easily grab those and pair them with a bit of hummus (page 57) instead of a bag of chips or some kind of sugary treat. Making hummus and cutting up veggies can be done quickly and the cleanup is simple. The other often overlooked bonus is that when it's time to snack, you won't find yourself mindlessly standing in front of the refrigerator wondering what to eat, allowing you to quickly get back to your other activities.

7. Cook up a big batch of rice or quinoa to keep in the refrigerator. Keeping rice or quinoa around when money is tight can really help extend whatever meals you prepare. For example, if you make a chili for the week, adding some rice or quinoa as you dish up a serving for yourself will help make that chili last longer. Besides stretching out the meals, saving you money, you also add more nutrition to the food.

8. Keep vegetable and citrus scraps. If you juice a lemon or lime for a recipe, don't just toss it when you're done. You can freeze and use it again when a recipe calls for the zest. Store-bought orange zest is expensive, so make it yourself. When you're done cutting up vegetables and have stems or other flavorful parts left over, freeze them. Once you have a good amount of frozen veggie scraps, make your own broth by boiling them with water in a pot (see page 16).

9. Don't store fresh herbs in the fridge. Instead of storing those fresh herbs in the damp, dark corners of your refrigerator, fill a mason jar with water and place the herbs in it. Set the jar in a sunny place in your kitchen. They will last weeks that way. Make sure you use separate jars for each herb and replace the water on occasion.

10. Use parchment paper or invest in a silicone baking mat. Parchment paper acts a great liner for baking. You can often reuse the same piece

many times over again, too, as it cleans up pretty easily. If you invest in a silicone baking mat, such as a Silpat, there will be no waste and you'll never need to use oil to grease the sheet. Nothing sticks to it. If you plan on doing high-heat roasting, I recommend using parchment paper instead (or check the recommended heat limits on your silicone baking mat).

11. Don't throw out those overripe bananas. Extra-ripe bananas can be used to make quick and healthy ice cream. Simply peel and freeze them in a ziplock bag (they should keep that way in the freezer for up to six months). Then take a frozen banana and 2 tablespoons of nut

butter of choice and blend until smooth. If you have a nut allergy, use sunflower butter. This method works great. My baby girl and I split one at least a few times a week.

12. Make packets for smoothies ahead of time. You can prep your fruits and veggies for smoothies and then place them into little baggies for the freezer. Then you just grab a bag and blend when you want a smoothie. Another option is to blend your smoothies and then freeze the mixture in ice cube trays. When you want a smoothie, simply pop out a few cubes and blend. It makes a quick and easy snack for the kids in the afternoon.

How to Handle Picky Eaters

f your kids are picky, I totally get it! My kids also have picky moments. When I first started my blog, I was giving my older daughter a typical American diet of processed foods. She had so many food fears from all the vomiting she experienced as a baby that I just fed her anything she wanted to eat. Nowadays, she enjoys fresh fruit and veggies, asks for salads, and loves my healthy desserts. My family is proof that even kids raised on a diet of processed foods can change. It may take a long time, as it did with my daughter, so patience is required. Here are some things I did with my girls.

1. Try making whole food versions of their favorite processed foods. I started to make mac and cheese with cashew cheese and whole grain pasta rather than the stuff in the blue box. Also, instead of making french fries using white potatoes, we started making them with sweet potato instead. Another staple in my household these days are pizzas made with whole grain flatbread.

2. When you go to the grocery store, let them pick out their own produce. My kids love to do this. They like that I'm giving them a say in what they eat.

3. Have them go through cookbooks and pick out meals for the family. This also makes them feel in control, and it really works. It helps them get excited about the meals they're going to eat!

4. If they're old enough, have them help prepare the meals. Not only are you teaching them valuable cooking skills, but they're more likely to eat food that they helped make. My five-year-old loves snacking on raw vegetables as I chop

them! Both my girls have been helping me since they were about eighteen months old. When my daughters were very small, I would give them very basic jobs, such as putting the veggies into a bowl. My older daughter used to say they were going "wee into the bowl!" (Oh, the silly things kids say.) Another simple job would be pressing the button on a food processor or blender. They both loved that simple task and seeing the machine start up.

5. Don't give up. Sometimes you have to put the same food in front of a child ten times (or more!) before he or she will actually try it. Don't give up the first time a healthy food is refused.

6. Limit snacking. If kids are snacking all day long, they won't be hungry at mealtimes. I usually let my girls have a couple of snacks a day, but that's it. As far as snacks go, I have a fruit bowl they can pick something out of.

7. Hide veggies in their food. I'm always hiding vegetables in my kids' food, whether it's tomato sauce (Hidden Veggies Tomato Sauce, page 168), smoothies (pages 185 to 202), or anything else I can think of.

8. Have patience with picky spouses or partners who are hesitant to come along on the healthy food journey. My family didn't just wake up eating whole foods one day, and it isn't really fair to think your partner will, either. Go slowly and don't get upset, but do keep testing new things. Try to reach a middle ground.

QUICK:
30 Minutes or Less

We're living in a fast-paced society where time is of the essence. Whether running the kids between all their activities or getting to work early to put the final additions on a presentation, we all wish we had more time. Cooking is usually one of the first things to go when we are pressed for time, especially with the numerous quick options on every corner. In this section, a little preparation will go a long way at every meal. Breakfasts (Maple Vanilla Baked Oatmeal Squares), sides (Cilantro Lime Cauliflower Rice), dinners (Lemon Basil Pasta with Cherry Tomatoes), and more can be made in 30 minutes or less. There's no reason to give up whole foods with these quick recipes.

SPINACH & MUSHROOM TOFU SCRAMBLE

ofu scrambles are like stir-fries for breakfast. You can basically throw in whatever you like (or whatever you have on hand) and it will just work. I love the combination of mushrooms and spinach here. The earthiness of the mushrooms and the sweet yet bitter flavor of the spinach pair well together. Feel free to add other veggies if you want. Red peppers and avocado would be a nice addition. You can eat this scramble as is, or serve it over toast. This doesn't last long in our house, so you might consider doubling the recipe.

1 In a large sauté pan, add the onion, garlic, and avocado oil. Cook on medium heat for 5 to 7 minutes, just long enough for the onions to soften.

2 Add the mushrooms, cover, and cook for another 5 minutes. Make sure to stir a couple times during this process.

3 Using your hands, crumble the tofu into the pan (see Note), then add the nutritional yeast. Stir well and cook for another 5 minutes.

4 Add the spinach, cover, and cook until the spinach starts to soften. Sprinkle in the salt.

5 Serve immediately or refrigerate for later. This should last in the fridge for at least a week (I don't recommend freezing it).

Makes 5 servings

Prep and cook time: 30 minutes

½ cup (80 g) diced yellow onion

2 teaspoons minced garlic (or 2 to 3 garlic cloves, minced)

2 tablespoons avocado oil (or olive oil)

3½ cups (225 g) sliced button mushrooms (about 8 ounces)

One 12-ounce (340 g) package extra-firm tofu, drained and patted dry

½ cup (30 g) nutritional yeast

3 cups (55 g) loosely packed baby spinach

1 teaspoon salt (or to taste)

Note

When crumbling the tofu, it's a good idea to cube it first. If you're holding the whole block while trying to crumble it, overly large chunks could fall into the pan. If that does happen, there's no need to panic or reach into the pan. Simply use a spatula to break it apart.

TOMATO BASIL CHICKPEA OMELETS

'll be honest—I used to struggle when it came to eating enough veggies. My solution: I work them into my breakfasts. A chickpea omelet is a great way to do just that. These "omelets" are almost more like pancakes, but they satisfy that craving for eggs. Plus, they feature one of my favorite ingredients: chickpea flour. You can use these chickpea omelets as a base and mix in a variety of vegetables, but my standby is this tomato basil version. They are best served fresh, and though they reheat well, some of the texture is lost when reheated.

1 In a large bowl, mix the water, chickpea flour, nutritional yeast, flaxseed meal, baking powder, salt, and turmeric.

2 Add the cherry tomatoes and basil to the bowl and combine.

3 Place a medium saucepan on medium-low heat. Pour a small amount of avocado oil into the pan.

4 Using a ½-cup (120 ml) measuring cup, scoop out some of the mixture and place it in the pan. Let it cook for several minutes. Much like a pancake, you'll be able to tell when it's ready to flip: The edges will bubble a bit and you should be able to get a spatula underneath easily. Once flipped, cook for another 1 to 2 minutes. When it's done, place the omelet on a serving dish.

5 Repeat the previous step until all the mixture is finished, adding more oil to the pan as needed.

6 Serve immediately or refrigerate for later. You can also freeze the omelets for up to 6 months.

Makes 6 omelets

Prep and cook time: 30 minutes

1 cup plus 1 tablespoon (255 ml) water

1 cup (110 g) chickpea flour

¼ cup (15 g) nutritional yeast

2 teaspoons flaxseed meal

1½ teaspoons baking powder

½ teaspoon salt (or to taste)

¼ teaspoon ground turmeric

1¼ cups (190 g) cherry tomatoes, halved

6 basil leaves

2 tablespoons avocado oil

Notes

* When I make this recipe, I make a big batch so I can have quick breakfasts all week.

* I like to eat my omelet with a side of roasted vegetables, but it can stand on its own as well.

MAPLE VANILLA BAKED OATMEAL SQUARES

Baked oatmeal squares are a good way to eat your oats on the go. With delicious maple syrup and vanilla, this recipe creates a wonderful morning pick-me-up that will keep you satisfied. It also makes a good treat for brunch. You can pack these in your kid's lunches, or carry them with you for an after-school or after-sports snack. This recipe is very adaptable to add in whatever you like—raisins or dried cranberries would work well, and maybe even some coconut shavings, too.

1 Preheat the oven to 350°F (180°C). Line an 8 x 8-inch (20 x 20 cm) glass baking dish with parchment paper. Make sure you leave a little paper sticking out of the sides. This will make it easier to remove the whole thing once it's baked.

2 In a large bowl, combine the oats, almonds, vanilla, cinnamon, and salt. Give the mixture a quick stir with a spatula.

3 Add the applesauce and maple syrup and mix until everything is well incorporated, about 1 minute by hand. Add the flax eggs and stir for another 30 seconds.

4 Transfer the mixture to the parchment-lined baking dish. Using your hands and the extra paper sticking out of the sides, press down on the mixture to pack it in well.

5 Bake in the oven for about 15 minutes, until the edges look golden.

6 Remove from the oven and let the baked oatmeal cool completely. Use a pizza cutter or knife to cut it into squares.

7 Store in the fridge in an airtight container. It should last about 2 weeks that way. You can also freeze it for up to 6 months.

Makes 9 large squares or 16 small squares

Prep and cook time: 20 minutes

---

3 cups (280 g) gluten-free rolled oats

½ cup (70 g) raw almonds

2 teaspoons ground vanilla beans (see Notes)

½ teaspoon ground cinnamon

½ teaspoon salt

½ cup (120 g) applesauce (see page 7)

½ cup (120 ml) maple syrup

2 flax eggs (see page 10)

Notes

- The ground vanilla beans really help give this oatmeal its strong flavor. You may use 2 teaspoons vanilla extract in place of the vanilla beans, but the flavor may not be as robust.

- You can also bake these in muffin tins for easy single servings. I find that making them in a baking dish works well for gatherings so people can pick their own size.

SWEET POTATO PANCAKES

'm always looking for ways to sneak veggies into my recipes. These pancakes are a perfect example: They're kid-friendly and healthy at the same time. They can be made ahead of time and frozen for a quick breakfast option as well. If I'm making these for a weekend breakfast, I spend 5 minutes preparing the dry ingredients the night before. Then I can quickly whip these up in the morning when I'm still groggy. Quickness seems to be an important thing when you're feeding hungry kids in the morning. Plus, with these pancakes, your kids will think they're eating dessert for breakfast. To make it an extra-special treat for the kids, add a handful of chocolate chips or top with a dollop of Coconut Whipped Cream (page 181) or pat of vegan butter.

1 In a large bowl, mix together all the dry ingredients.

2 In a medium bowl, mix all of the wet ingredients except the coconut oil.

3 Add the dry ingredients to the wet ingredients and mix until just combined. I use a spatula and do this by hand, but you can use a stand mixer if you prefer.

4 Heat a large sauté pan on medium heat. Add the coconut oil. Using a ¼-cup (60 ml) measuring scoop, drop the batter onto the sauté pan. Once you see the edges start to brown a little, you know it's ready to flip (1 to 2 minutes). Repeat until the batter is used up.

5 Serve immediately or, once cool, refrigerate or freeze for later use. These should last for 2 weeks in the fridge and up to 6 months in the freezer.

Makes 8 to 10 pancakes

Prep and cook time: 25 minutes

---

2 cups (210 g) gluten-free oat flour

2 teaspoons baking powder

1 teaspoon ground cinnamon

½ teaspoon ground ginger

½ teaspoon salt

¼ teaspoon ground nutmeg

1½ cups (360 ml) almond milk

1 cup (240 ml) sweet potato purée (see Note)

2 flax eggs (see page 10)

2 tablespoons maple syrup

1 teaspoon vanilla extract

2 tablespoons melted coconut oil

Note

To make the sweet potato purée, peel and cube 1 large sweet potato or 2 small sweet potatoes, then place them in a large pot of boiling water. Boil until soft, 15 to 20 minutes. Drain the water and place the sweet potatoes back in the pot. Use an immersion blender or potato masher to purée the sweet potatoes. This step can be done in advance. It should keep in the fridge for about 2 weeks. You can also freeze it for up to 6 months.

ORANGE GINGER BEET RICE

The beet is one of those vegetables people either love or hate. I happen to love them almost any way they're prepared. Sometimes making great-tasting food is just about keeping it simple and letting the flavors of the few ingredients you use stand out and shine. The citrus in this dish adds a nice tanginess, and, as a result, it goes perfectly with the beets. If you like beets and ginger, this dish is for you.

1 In a food processor, add the roughly chopped beets and pulse until you see a rice-like consistency, 1 to 2 minutes. If you have a smaller food processor (a 7-cup food processor or smaller), you may need to process the beets in two batches.

2 Add the beets and avocado oil to a large sauté pan. Cook on medium heat, stirring often, for about 5 minutes. Then add the orange juice, garlic, ginger, orange zest, and salt and continue to cook for another 3 to 4 minutes so the flavors develop.

3 Remove from the heat and garnish with slivered almonds, fresh parsley, and green onions. Serve immediately or refrigerate for later (it should last up to 3 days in the fridge).

Makes 4 servings

Prep and cook time: 30 minutes

2 large beets, peeled and roughly chopped

2 tablespoons avocado oil

Juice of 1 large orange (or ¼ cup [60 ml] orange juice)

2 to 3 garlic cloves, minced

1 teaspoon minced fresh ginger

1 teaspoon grated orange zest

½ teaspoon salt (or more to taste)

¼ cup (30 g) slivered almonds

¼ cup (15 g) freshly chopped flat-leaf parsley

2 tablespoons chopped green onions

ARUGULA SALAD WITH APPLES & FENNEL

In the same family as broccoli, arugula is an incredible vegetable associated with lowering your risk of cancer, and just two cups of arugula contain 50 percent of your recommended daily intake of vitamin K. This is truly a wonderful little leaf. Fennel, a plant with a licorice-like flavor, has been used in natural remedies since ancient times and is used in a variety of ways today given its versatile bulb, foliage, and seeds. The apples bring everything together with their sweet crunchiness. This salad has such an amazing flavor that you'll forget you're eating a healthy dish.

1. Add all the salad ingredients to a large serving bowl.

2. In a small bowl, whisk together the dressing ingredients.

3. Pour the dressing over the salad and toss it until evenly coated.

4. If using the fennel fronds, chop them and add as garnish. Serve immediately.

Variation

Another great dressing to try with this salad is the Creamy Avocado & Cilantro Dressing (page 173). It offers a slightly different take on the same recipe.

Makes 3 to 4 servings
Prep time: 10 minutes

SALAD

5 cups (100 g) loosely packed arugula

1 apple, diced

1 cup (150 g) halved cherry tomatoes

1 cup (130 g) peeled and chopped cucumber

½ cup (50 g) thinly sliced fennel bulb, with any wilted outer layers removed (reserve the fennel fronds for garnish, if desired)

¼ cup (40 g) pepitas (pumpkin seeds)

DRESSING

2 tablespoons olive oil (or avocado oil)

2 tablespoons lemon juice

½ teaspoon salt (or to taste)

SWEET & SPICY WARM PEPPER SALAD

This salad features bell peppers of all kinds, making it a colorful addition to any summer pool party. For the spice, use whatever kind of spicy pepper you and your guests can handle. The recipe calls for two serrano chile peppers, which are the thin green ones 2 to 4 inches (5 to 10 cm) in length. They make the salad a bit spicy but still tolerable to most people. If you don't like spicy food, don't fret—simply remove the seeds (which are the hottest part), or omit the spicy peppers all together.

1 In a pan on medium-low heat, sauté the serrano chile pepper in the avocado oil for 2 to 3 minutes.

2 Reduce the heat to the lowest setting and mix in the other ingredients. Sauté for 4 to 5 minutes. The peppers should be crunchy but warmed through.

3 Place the contents of the pan in a bowl and serve immediately. This should keep for at least a week in the fridge. It's also just as tasty served cold.

Makes 5 to 6 servings

Prep and cook time: 25 minutes

2 serrano chile peppers, diced

1 teaspoon avocado oil

2 cups (300 g) sweet corn kernels (2 ears sweet corn)

2 cups (330 g) chopped mango (about 1 mango)

1 red bell pepper, chopped

1 yellow bell pepper, chopped

1 green bell pepper, chopped

1 orange bell pepper, chopped

½ teaspoon minced garlic (or 1 garlic clove, minced)

½ teaspoon ground coriander

½ teaspoon salt (or to taste)

Notes

- If you do this just right, the spice level should be tolerable to those who don't like the heat of a raw chile pepper.

- If you have leftovers, be sure to use a slotted spoon to move them to a storage container, as the mango releases a lot of liquid.

- If you're going to refrigerate this immediately for later enjoyment, let it cool completely before covering the container, or else it will steam up in the refrigerator and become a soggy mess.

MOROCCAN CARROT SALAD

This Moroccan carrot salad is an easy recipe for the beginner cook and a perfect summer meal. It has wonderful, uniquely bold flavors that make it stand out. Since it's raw and doesn't involve any actual cooking, it can be prepared quickly.

1 Mix together all the ingredients in a large serving bowl.

2 Serve immediately or refrigerate for later. The flavors will develop even more the longer it sits. This salad should last for about a week in the fridge.

Variations

* If dates prove too hard to come by, raisins are a great substitute. Use about 2 tablespoons.

* If you wanted to make this more of a main dish, you could add 1 cup (165 g) chickpeas. You'll also be adding some protein that way.

Makes 4 servings

Prep time: 20 minutes

3 cups (330 g) shredded carrots (about 8 medium carrots, shredded)

⅔ cup (80 g) thinly sliced red onion

2 Medjool dates, pitted and chopped (see Variations)

2 tablespoons lemon juice (or the juice of 1 small lemon)

1 tablespoon freshly chopped flat-leaf parsley

1 tablespoon freshly chopped mint

½ teaspoon ground cinnamon

1 teaspoon ground coriander

½ teaspoon salt (or to taste)

MASSAGED KALE & CHICKPEA SALAD

Kale is the one of the most popular leafy green vegetables for health buffs. Some people, however, have an issue with the taste. Raw kale can be chewy and bitter, especially for picky eaters. Massaging kale helps it wilt, turning it darker green, making it easier to chew, and giving it a sweeter flavor. If you haven't tried this technique before, you'll be amazed at the transformation before your eyes. If you're unsure whether the massage worked, just take a bite. Keep massaging if it's still too fibrous.

1 Remove the kale leaves from the stems and place the leaves in a large bowl. Once all the stems are removed, rip the leaves into bite-size pieces. Next, begin to massage the kale by using your hands to scrunch up the leaves. Do this for about 2 minutes until the kale begins to soften.

2 Once the kale is massaged, add the chickpeas, red onion, and parsley to the bowl.

3 In a small bowl, mix together the lemon juice, balsamic vinegar, pomegranate molasses, minced garlic, and salt to make the dressing.

4 Pour the dressing over the salad and mix for about a minute, until everything looks well combined.

5 Serve immediately or refrigerate for later. Personally, I think this salad gets better as it sits in the fridge. It should last for about 4 to 5 days in the fridge.

Makes 4 servings
Prep time: 20 minutes

SALAD

10 to 12 curly kale leaves

4 cups (650 g) cooked chickpeas (see Notes)

⅓ cup (50 g) thinly sliced red onion

3 tablespoons freshly chopped flat-leaf parsley

DRESSING

Juice of 1 medium lemon (or 2 tablespoons lemon juice)

1 tablespoon balsamic vinegar

1 tablespoon pomegranate molasses (see Notes)

1 garlic clove, minced

¼ teaspoon salt (or to taste)

Notes

* Save the kale stems for juicing or for vegetable broth (see page 16).

* If you cook dried chickpeas, measure out 2 cups (400 g) dried chickpeas.

* If you can't find pomegranate molasses, you can substitute with 1 tablespoon balsamic vinegar plus 1 teaspoon of maple syrup.

SWEET CORN SALAD WITH ARUGULA

I love sweet corn—I feel like a kid in a candy store as I shuck and boil it during the summer season. Sweet corn is typically a non-GMO crop, unlike its cousin field corn, which has a more industrial use. This recipe combines the goodness of sweet corn with the peppery flavor of arugula and the earthiness of thyme. I don't eat a lot of thyme, but it transforms this dish, so don't omit it. Try it and I'm sure you won't be disappointed.

1 Remove the husks, silk, and ends from the corn.

2 Fill a large stockpot with water and bring to a boil. Add the corn and boil for 7 to 10 minutes. The corn will turn bright yellow when done.

3 Remove the corn and wait for it to cool, about 10 minutes.

4 Using a serrated knife, remove the corn kernels from the cobs.

5 Place the kernels in a large serving bowl with the remaining ingredients and mix well.

6 Serve immediately or refrigerate for later. The salad gets better the longer it sits. It should last at least a week in the fridge.

Makes 4 servings

Prep and cook time: 25 minutes

6 ears sweet corn (see Note)

2 to 3 cups (40 to 60 g) loosely packed arugula, roughly chopped

2 to 3 tablespoons white wine vinegar

1 teaspoon dried thyme

½ teaspoon salt (or to taste)

¼ teaspoon ground black pepper

Variation

Cherry tomatoes and avocado would make a nice addition to this salad. If you decide to add them, I suggest using 1 cup (150 g) cherry tomatoes and 1 small avocado, sliced.

Note

If you want to save time, you could use frozen corn kernels in this and cook according to the package instead of boiling 7 to 10 minutes. Some of the fresh crunchiness of the corn will be lost, though.

CILANTRO LIME CAULIFLOWER RICE

If you haven't tried cauliflower rice before, it's life changing! I'm not even a huge fan of cauliflower, but I love cauliflower rice. You're probably thinking, *What is cauliflower rice?* Well, it's when you pulse cauliflower florets in a food processor to give it the appearance of rice. Once it's cooked, the texture is pretty similar to rice, too. I find the best way to flavor cauliflower rice is with a mild seasoning, as heavy sauces tend to turn it to mush. It makes a perfect side dish for any meal and is a great alternative to rice for those who are avoiding grains.

1 In a food processor, add half of the florets and gently pulse a few times. You want to break up the cauliflower into rice-size pieces, not process it into mush. Put it in a bowl and repeat with the other half of the cauliflower.

2 Add the cauliflower to a large sauté pan with the avocado oil and garlic. Sauté on medium heat for about 5 minutes, until the cauliflower is toasty and slightly browned.

3 Place the cauliflower in a large serving bowl and add the remaining ingredients. Mix well.

4 Serve immediately for optimal results. This should last about 4 to 5 days in the fridge but probably won't freeze well.

Makes 5 to 6 servings

Prep and cook time: 20 minutes

1 head cauliflower, cut into florets

2 tablespoons avocado oil (see Note)

1 or 2 garlic cloves, minced

2 tablespoons freshly chopped cilantro

2 tablespoons lime juice (or the juice of 1 lime)

1 tablespoon freshly chopped flat-leaf parsley

1 teaspoon salt (or to taste)

½ teaspoon dried oregano

Variation

This dish is excellent with avocado slices on top.

Note

I use avocado oil because I like the flavor it adds, but you can use another oil if you prefer. Olive oil or coconut oil would work well, too. If you don't use oils, you can cook the cauliflower in a little water instead.

LEMON BASIL PASTA WITH CHERRY TOMATOES

There's something so comforting about pasta dishes. This Lemon Basil Pasta is no exception. I simply love how all the flavors come together in this dish. The lemon freshens everything up while the tomatoes keep the flavors traditional, and the basil and capers add sweet and sour bursts that excite your senses. This meal can be made pretty quickly, but make sure to not overcook the pasta.

1 In a large sauté pan (or large pot), bring the water to a boil. Once the water is boiling, add the pasta.

2 Cook the pasta for 7 to 10 minutes, stirring as often as needed to be sure the pasta stays separated. Once the pasta looks mostly cooked (slightly less than al dente), remove from the heat and drain, cover the pasta, and set it aside.

3 In the same pan you cooked the spaghetti, add the tomatoes, lemon juice, olive oil, and garlic and cook for 2 to 3 minutes.

4 Once the mixture is heated through, stir in the spaghetti. Cook partially covered on low heat for 5 to 7 minutes. Check and stir a few times to be sure the pasta does not stick to the bottom of the pan or overcook.

5 Remove from the heat and stir in the basil, green onion, and capers. Season with salt.

6 This dish is best served immediately, garnished with basil leaves, if desired. It will last at least a week in the fridge (if you even have leftovers). I don't recommend freezing it.

Makes 3 to 4 servings

Prep and cook time: 30 minutes

6 cups (1.4 L) water

One 8-ounce (227 g) package quinoa spaghetti (see Note)

1 pint (about 2 cups [300 g]) cherry tomatoes, halved

¼ cup (60 ml) lemon juice (or the juice of 1 large lemon)

1 tablespoon olive oil

1 garlic clove, minced

⅔ cup (30 g) freshly chopped basil, plus extra leaves for garnish, optional

2 tablespoons chopped green onions

1 tablespoon capers

1 teaspoon salt (or to taste)

Note

I used quinoa pasta for this recipe, but you can use any pasta you like. I do recommend staying away from brown rice pasta, though, as it seems to fall apart and clump while cooking. If you choose to use whole wheat pasta, you'll probably need to cook it a minute or two longer. You can make this grain-free by using zucchini pasta: Simply spiralize two zucchini and give them a quick sauté with all the ingredients, just a minute or two, to warm it up and let the basil wilt slightly.

SWEET POTATO PASTA WITH SPINACH & TOMATOES

The spiralized sweet potatoes give a bit of heartiness to a light dish. The spinach adds some great flavors, and its nutritional benefits can't be emphasized enough—it's a good source of iron, boosts skin and bone health, and the list just keeps going. The tomatoes help round out this dish, making it a truly delicious treat. And while it doesn't necessarily seem like a lot of food, it will leave you full for quite some time. If you're new to spiralizing, this dish will make you feel good about getting a spiralizer. To save some time, spiralize the sweet potatoes in advance.

1 Spiralize the sweet potatoes with a spiralizer. Set aside.

2 In a large sauté pan on medium heat, add the olive oil, onions, and garlic. Cover and cook for 5 to 7 minutes, stirring occasionally.

3 Add the spinach, cover, and cook for a few more minutes, just until the spinach starts to wilt.

4 Add the sweet potatoes and cherry tomatoes and cook for another 3 to 4 minutes, until soft.

5 Garnish with the pepitas and hemp hearts. For best results, serve immediately. This should last in the fridge for 4 to 5 days.

Makes 4 servings

Prep and cook time: 30 minutes

2 small sweet potatoes (about 6 ounces [170 g]), peeled

2 tablespoons olive oil

1 onion, thinly sliced

2 garlic cloves, minced

5 ounces (140 g) baby spinach

2 cups (300 g) halved cherry tomatoes

¼ cup (30 g) pepitas (pumpkin seeds)

2 tablespoons hemp hearts

1 teaspoon salt (or to taste)

Variations

* If you want some additional protein in this, you can add 2 cups (330 g) cooked chickpeas or 2 cups (340 g) cooked black beans.

* If you don't own a spiralizer, you can make this dish with brown rice pasta or quinoa pasta. Cook according to the package, skip the sweet potato, and toss everything with the pasta before garnishing.

* I think fresh basil would be a nice addition. If you decide to use it, I suggest ¼ cup (4 g) loosely packed basil. You can add it at the same time as the spinach.

CHEESY GARLIC POPCORN

Popcorn is a big hit at our house, especially with the kids. Like any snack, though, the popcorn you find at most grocery stores is not very good for you, containing fake butters and artificial flavors. Before the microwave came along, the stove was the most common way to make popcorn, and this is the method I prefer when making popcorn for my family. I also like to use organic kernels. This is a great snack when you're on the go; just throw a bag into the car and off you go into the sunset, easy-peasy.

1 In a large stockpot, add the coconut oil and 1 popcorn kernel. Cover and put the heat on medium-high.

2 Once you hear the kernel pop, add the rest of the kernels and place the cover on the pot. Pick the pot up and shake it constantly until all the kernels are popped.

3 Once all the kernels are popped, turn off the heat, remove the cover, add the remaining ingredients, and stir well. This is best if eaten immediately.

Makes 4 cups (40 g)

Prep and cook time: 15 minutes

- 2 tablespoons melted coconut oil
- ¼ cup (50 g) popcorn kernels
- 2 tablespoons nutritional yeast
- 1 teaspoon salt (or to taste)
- ½ teaspoon garlic powder

Variation

If you want a sweet version, you can omit the nutritional yeast and garlic powder, then add 2 tablespoons maple syrup and 1 teaspoon ground cinnamon.

AVOCADO & CHICKPEA STUFFED CUCUMBERS

This recipe is easy to make, but the presentation will still wow your dinner guests. Best served as an appetizer, these little bite-size stuffed cucumbers pack a lot of flavor with minimal effort. Before you start, be sure you have some toothpicks on hand, as they not only help the cucumbers keep their shape, but also allow your dinner guests to pick them up without much mess.

1 Peel and cut the cucumbers down the middle lengthwise, splitting them into two pieces.

2 Using a vegetable peeler or mandoline, slice the cucumbers lengthwise down the middle, from one end to the other. Put the strips aside.

3 Place the remaining ingredients in the food processor and pulse until small chunks form. You may need to scrape down the sides a few times.

4 Lay a cucumber strip flat on a cutting board and spread some of the stuffing on one end.

5 Roll the cucumber up. You can place a toothpick in the roll to keep it together.

6 Repeat steps 4 and 5 until all the cucumber strips are used. There will be stuffing left over (see Notes).

7 Serve immediately—these are best made and eaten quickly (as they sit, the cucumber tends to get soggy).

Makes 30 cucumber rolls

Prep time: 20 minutes

2 medium cucumbers (see Notes)

3 cups (500 g) cooked chickpeas

2 avocados, pitted and peeled

2 tablespoons lemon juice (or the juice of 1 lemon)

1 tablespoon freshly chopped flat-leaf parsley

1 garlic clove, minced

1 teaspoon salt (or to taste)

Notes

- Although the recipe is written for two cucumbers, there's enough stuffing to make many more of these. If you don't plan on using more cucumbers, the stuffing works well as a sandwich spread or just eaten plain by the spoonful.

- There will also be a good amount of cucumber scraps. There's no need to throw these away; in my house we cut up the scraps and add them to a salad.

SRIRACHA & LIME KALE CHIPS

K ale chips seem to be all the rage these days. I first made them as one of my go-to snacks when I started eating a whole food diet. This spicy version is for all those people who get turned off by the sight of kale. A light coating with a bit of sriracha and lime juice add a flavor spicy-food lovers won't be able to pass up. If you like heat, these are right up your alley; if heat isn't your thing, replace the sriracha with a roasted red pepper sauce in its place. Either version will delight your senses.

1 Preheat the oven to 300°F (150°C). Line a baking sheet with parchment paper.

2 Place the kale pieces the baking sheet.

3 Mix the sriracha and lime juice together in a small bowl.

4 Using a silicone brush, coat each kale piece with the sriracha-lime mixture.

5 Bake for 20 to 22 minutes, until the chips are crispy.

6 To keep any extra chips crispy, store them in an airtight container with rice scattered on the bottom (the rice will absorb moisture). The chips should last at least 4 days in a container in the pantry.

Variation

Another delicious way to enjoy kale chips is to use a mix of white balsamic vinegar and avocado oil. In a small bowl, mix together ¼ cup (60 ml) white balsamic vinegar and 1 tablespoon avocado oil. Brush the mixture onto each kale chip. Then sprinkle with a little salt. Bake as directed. So good!

Makes 2 to 3 servings

Prep and cook time: 30 minutes

6 to 7 kale leaves, stems removed, cut or torn into 4-inch (10 cm) pieces

¼ cup (60 ml) sriracha

2 tablespoons lime juice (or the juice of 1 lime)

CUCUMBER DILL HUMMUS

Hummus is always great for a healthy snack. It's also one of the easiest things to make yourself, is inexpensive, and even freezes well. There's really no reason to buy store-bought brands. All varieties and flavors of hummus are eaten in my household, but this particular dill and cucumber combo is near and dear to my heart. Dill is one of those herbs that just seems to light up everything it touches. My personal favorite pairing with hummus is, of course, raw veggies such as carrots and red bell peppers.

1 Place the chickpeas, cucumber, and dill in a food processor. Blend for 1 minute.

2 Add the remaining ingredients except the water and olive oil and blend until smooth, 1 to 2 minutes.

3 Add the water 1 tablespoon at a time, until you reach your desired consistency. It should be very creamy.

4 Serve immediately or refrigerate for later. This hummus should last at least a week in the fridge. You can also freeze it for up to 3 months.

Makes 2 cups (500 g)

Prep time: 10 minutes

1½ cups (250 g) cooked chickpeas (or one 15-ounce [425 g] can of chickpeas, drained and rinsed)

¾ cup (100 g) peeled and chopped cucumber

¼ cup (8 g) freshly chopped dill

¼ cup (75 g) tahini (see Variations)

2 garlic cloves, minced

1½ teaspoons ground cumin

Juice of 1 lemon (2 to 3 tablespoons lemon juice)

½ teaspoon salt (or to taste)

1 to 3 tablespoons water

1 tablespoon olive oil, optional (see Variations)

Variations

* If you don't like tahini or can't find it, you can use sunflower butter instead. Some people also just omit the tahini altogether, although I personally don't recommend it, since it adds such great flavor to the hummus.

* If you want, you can drizzle about 1 tablespoon olive oil over the hummus right before serving it. The olive oil adds more flavor and also makes a pretty presentation. You can also sprinkle some extra cumin on top, if you like.

APRICOT ALMOND ENERGY BITES

Right after a workout, I always eat some type of snack with nuts and fruit. It could be anything from apples and almond butter, a date stuffed with cashew butter, or a handful of dried fruits and nuts. The snacks are usually small, compact, and full of protein. This snack encompasses all of the above, and it's a cinch to make, with only four ingredients. The dried apricots and almonds complement each other's unique flavors. These travel quite well and make a great homemade snack on the road.

① In a food processor, combine the almonds and cinnamon. Blend for 1 minute.

② Add the apricots and blend for about 2 minutes.

③ Slowly add the water, a little at a time, until you see the mixture start to clump together.

④ Once the mixture is ready, roll it into bite-size balls. The dough will be a bit sticky, so using wet hands helps.

⑤ Set the balls on a parchment paper–lined baking sheet or plate and place them in the fridge to firm up. It should take about 10 minutes.

⑥ These snack balls should last at least 2 weeks in the fridge. You can also freeze them for up to 6 months.

Makes 20 snack bites

Prep and chill time: 20 minutes

1½ cups (210 g) raw almonds (see Notes)

1 teaspoon ground cinnamon

1¼ cups (165 g) dried apricots (see Notes)

2 to 4 tablespoons water

Notes

* The nuts and dried fruits are substitutable in this recipe. Any nut/fruit combo will work as long as you use dried fruits (as opposed to fresh).

* If you have a nut allergy, you can use sunflower seeds in place of the almonds.

CINNAMON-SPICED BAKED PEARS

hese baked pears are simply amazing. Pears release so much sugar when baked that you'll think you're eating candy. The cinnamon and nutmeg add a bit of spice. As an added benefit, pears are actually higher in fiber content than their apple cousins, so this isn't a total loss in terms of health. I recommend leaving the skin on the pears, as it helps hold the pears together under the heat of baking. If you don't have or don't like pecans, walnuts or almonds are also great to use.

1 Preheat the oven to 350°F (180°C).

2 Cut the pears in half lengthwise and then remove the cores (I used a melon baller to do this).

3 Slice a small sliver off the back of each pear half to create a flat surface so they can sit in a baking dish without sliding around.

4 Place all the pears face up in a baking dish. I use a 9 x 13-inch (23 x 33 cm) baking dish (the pears may not fit in anything smaller).

5 Fill the center of each pear with the pecan pieces and raisins, then drizzle 1 teaspoon of the maple syrup over each pear half. Sprinkle with cinnamon and a pinch of nutmeg.

6 Bake the pears for about 25 minutes, until the sugar begins to caramelize.

7 Serve while still warm. Keep any leftovers up to a week in the fridge.

Makes 8 pear halves

Prep and cook time: 30 minutes

4 Bosc, Anjou, or Bartlett pears

½ cup (60 g) pecan pieces (see Variations)

¼ cup (40 g) raisins

2 to 3 tablespoons maple syrup

1 teaspoon ground cinnamon

Pinch of ground nutmeg

Variations

* These would be great topped with Coconut Whipped Cream (page 181) or Salted Caramel Sauce (page 182).

* If you need a nut-free option, you can use gluten-free rolled oats instead of pecans.

CHOCOLATE PEANUT BUTTER COOKIES

I f you've been trying to get your kids to eat more beans, then you must try these chocolate peanut butter cookies. They're flourless thanks to the black beans, and they also provide a good boost of unexpected protein and fiber. My kids love these and have never suspected the main ingredient. All you taste is chocolate and peanut-buttery goodness. This recipe makes a great start for kids transitioning to a whole food, plant-based diet, too.

1 Preheat the oven to 350°F (180°C). Line two baking sheets with parchment paper.

2 Add all the ingredients except the chocolate chips to a food processor and mix until smooth, about 2 minutes. You may have to scrape down the sides a few times. The mixture will be very thick.

3 Using a medium cookie scoop or a couple of spoons, drop the cookies onto the baking sheets, about 1 inch (2.5 cm) apart.

4 Flatten each cookie slightly with the palm of your hand. If you choose to garnish with the chocolate chips, do so now.

5 Bake for 10 minutes. Let the cookies cool for about 10 minutes before removing from the baking sheet. Store in an airtight container.

Makes 20 cookies

Prep and cook time: 30 minutes

1½ cups (255 g) cooked black beans (or one 15-ounce [425 g] can black beans, drained and rinsed)

1 cup (270 g) unsalted peanut butter (see Variations)

½ cup (40 g) cocoa powder

½ cup (120 ml) maple syrup

2 teaspoons vanilla extract

1 teaspoon baking powder

½ teaspoon salt

⅓ cup (60 g) chocolate chips for the tops of the cookies, optional

Variations

- You can use a different nut butter if you want; I suggest almond or cashew butter.

- If you have a nut allergy, you can use sunflower butter as a substitute.

- If you use salted peanut butter, then omit the salt, although the cookies still might turn out a bit too salty.

BLACKBERRY ICE CREAM

Nothing compares to homemade ice cream. Not only is it much cheaper to make it yourself, but you can also control the ingredients that go into it. One of my favorite kitchen gadgets is my ice cream maker. If you eat ice cream regularly, an ice cream maker will save you money within just a few batches. Most store-bought ice creams are expensive and have unnecessary fillers and additives to keep them shelf-stable. On the other hand, this healthy ice cream recipe contains just five simple ingredients. Plus it becomes a family affair while we all sit around the ice cream maker waiting to get a taste of our next concoction—the experience is more than just a tasty treat! (Just make sure the bowl has been chilled in the freezer for at least 24 hours before attempting this recipe.) This recipe produces a soft-serve ice cream. If you like a harder ice cream, add 1 teaspoon vodka just before you blend all the ingredients together to keep it from becoming a solid block when you freeze it.

Makes 4 cups (960 ml)

Prep and chill time: 25 minutes

One 13.5-ounce (400 ml) can full-fat coconut milk (see Notes)

1 pint (about 2 cups [340 g]) fresh blackberries, plus a few more for mixing in (see Notes)

3 tablespoons maple syrup

1 vanilla bean, cut open and seeds scraped out (see Notes)

Pinch of salt

1 In a blender, mix all the ingredients for at least 1 minute.

2 Pour the contents into the properly chilled bowl of your ice cream maker.

3 Turn the ice cream maker on. It should take about 20 minutes to make a soft-serve ice cream. When there are 5 minutes left, add a handful of whole blackberries. Use a spatula to guide the ice cream around so the blackberries mix in evenly.

4 Serve immediately for soft-serve ice cream, or place in the freezer for 1 hour to make a harder ice cream. Store in the freezer in an air-tight tub. This should last up to 6 months in the freezer.

Notes

* If you use almond milk or another nondairy milk rather than full-fat coconut milk, this will be icy in texture.

* If you want to use frozen blackberries, let them thaw first.

* Use only the vanilla seeds. You can use ½ teaspoon vanilla extract instead of a vanilla bean.

CHOCOLATE ESPRESSO PUDDING

Coffee and chocolate were just made for each other, as you'll see in this super-rich pudding recipe. I add a few chocolate chips to make it even more of a treat. The secret ingredient, avocado, gives it a rich and velvety texture. Plus the avocado contains healthy fats and other added health benefits (did you know the avocado contains more potassium than a banana?). You won't really know the avocado is there, either, because the coffee and chocolate combination mask the flavor entirely. Learning secrets like this makes vegan cooking easier and allows you to think of other ways you can utilize the same tricks.

Makes 4 servings
Prep time: 15 minutes

2 ripe avocados, pitted and peeled

⅓ cup (35 g) cocoa powder

⅓ cup (80 ml) maple syrup

¼ cup (45 g) chocolate chips

1 teaspoon coffee extract (see Notes)

1 In a high-power blender or food processor, blend the avocados until there are no lumps. This can take several minutes, and you may need to stop and scrape down the sides a few times.

2 Add the remaining ingredients and blend until smooth. This should take about 5 minutes, and you may need to scrape down the sides a few times here, too.

3 Serve immediately or refrigerate for later. This should last about 4 days in the fridge.

Notes

* This recipe calls for coffee extract, which may be located in the baking section of most grocery stores. If you can't find coffee extract, you can also use 1 teaspoon instant coffee granules for a similar flavor.

* This recipe is wonderful topped with homemade Coconut Whipped Cream (page 181).

EASY:
Effortless Slow Cooker Dishes

A slow cooker is an amazing way to make great food with little effort—be it a soup, chili, or even breakfast. These recipes are sure to please even the pickiest eaters while freeing up your time. The best part? All the while, these recipes will be filling your home with the delectable smells that only slow cookers can create. So try the Corn Chowder or the Apple Cinnamon Quinoa and experience how effortless yummy can be.

APPLE CINNAMON QUINOA

I t doesn't get much easier than slow cooker meals, since most of the time you can just throw everything in the slow cooker, turn it on, and walk away. As an added bonus, with this recipe your house will smell amazing, just like a cinnamon candle! The quinoa gives this dish loads of protein, so you can feel good about eating it. I recommend making this on the weekend and then storing it in serving-size containers for an easy, on-the-go breakfast option all week. Serve with fresh fruit and almond milk, or on its own.

1 Combine all the ingredients in a slow cooker and stir well. Cover and cook on high for 3 hours or on low for 6 hours.

2 Serve immediately or refrigerate for later.

Variations

- If you don't want to use quinoa, you can use gluten-free steel-cut oats instead. It's an equal swap.

- If you're like me and love the combination of apples and almond butter, top each serving with a bit of almond butter.

- A drizzle of Salted Caramel Sauce (page 182) would be delicious and add a little more protein.

- You can also try adding pepitas (pumpkin seeds), hemp hearts, or chia seeds. I recommend about 2 tablespoons as a starting point.

Note

To make this on the stove, put all the ingredients into a large pot, bring to a boil, and then turn down the heat. Cook until all the liquid is absorbed (this usually takes 15 to 20 minutes).

Makes 6 servings

Prep and cook time: 3 hours 10 minutes to 6 hours 10 minutes

3 cups (720 ml) almond milk or water

1¾ cups (300 g) uncooked quinoa (see Variations)

2 apples, chopped (preferably Gala)

½ cup (80 g) raisins or chopped Medjool dates

1½ teaspoons ground cinnamon

½ teaspoon salt

¼ teaspoon ground ginger

¼ teaspoon ground nutmeg

ONION SOUP

This is our vegan take on French onion soup. A classic French onion soup uses beef broth, cheese, and more cheese. Our version uses vegetable broth, plenty of onions, and some other great ingredients. This soup will be a wonderful addition to your kitchen. Onions have some great cardiovascular health benefits, and low-heat cooking allows their nutrients to stay intact. The real secret for this soup is slicing the onions as thin as you can, whether you use a mandoline or a sharp knife. Try not to peel too many of the outer layers, though, as a good amount of the nutrients sits just under the paper-like outer covering. The other secret to this recipe is time—making the slow cooker an integral part of the dish.

1 Combine all the ingredients in a slow cooker, cover, and cook on high for 6 hours. When it's done, remove the bay leaves.

2 Serve immediately or refrigerate for later. This should last a week in the fridge, or you can freeze it for up to 6 months.

Note

Add a dollop of Cashew Cream (page 175) or Macadamia Nut Cheese Sauce (page 171) on top for extra creaminess.

Makes 5 to 6 servings

Prep and cook time: 6 hours 20 minutes

---

6 cups (1.4 L) vegetable broth (see page 16)

3 large yellow onions, thinly sliced

2 bay leaves

¼ cup (60 ml) balsamic vinegar

1 teaspoon dried sage

1 teaspoon dried thyme

1 teaspoon salt (or to taste)

VEGGIE ENCHILADA SOUP

Enchilada soup, much like tortilla soup, is a Southwestern favorite normally made a little on the spicy side, with chicken and loads of cheese. The essence of this soup isn't found in the chicken or the cheese, though—the real heart is the peppers. This version leaves out the chicken and cheese, opting to include more veggies in their place. The soup comes out thick and will definitely warm the soul. The roasted red peppers and roasted tomatoes bring a ton a flavor to the base, while the yellow chile peppers add a real kick. Since this is made in a slow cooker, there's not a lot of preparation time, either. You can put everything together in the morning, start the slow cooker, and come back from work that evening with an amazing soup that's ready to eat.

1. Place all the ingredients in a slow cooker. Cover and cook on high for 6 hours.

2. Serve immediately or refrigerate for later. This should last a week in the fridge, and you can freeze it for up to 3 months.

Variations

* Although this recipe doesn't call for vegan cheese sauce (page 171), its creaminess would go very well in this soup. If you want, you can add it right before you serve the soup.

* A great topper on this recipe would be some avocado chunks. You can place a bit of parsley or cilantro on top for presentation, too.

Note

If you want some good pepper flavor without the heat, try using bell peppers or, if in season, Hatch chile peppers.

Makes 6 to 7 servings

Prep and cook time: 6 hours 20 minutes

4 cups (720 g) roughly chopped roasted red tomatoes (see page 15)

2 cups (300 g) sweet corn kernels

2 cups (300 g) roughly chopped roasted red peppers (see page 15)

2 cups (480 ml) vegetable broth (see page 16)

1 yellow onion, chopped

1 to 2 yellow chile peppers, roughly chopped (see Note)

2 garlic cloves, minced

1 teaspoon chili powder

1 teaspoon ground cumin

½ teaspoon ground coriander

1 to 2 teaspoons salt (or to taste)

HEARTY THREE-BEAN SOUP

Bean soups are a fantastic way to use up leftover vegetables. For the beginner cook, they're also really easy to get right. The beans in this recipe are substitutable, so you can use whatever kinds you happen to have on hand. Other vegetables can also be added without much change to the soup overall. The nicest part of bean soups is that they turn out so hearty. They're high in protein and fiber, too, so you're sure to stay full for a long time. It also doesn't hurt that they're pretty cheap to make, so if you're on a budget, soups like this one are perfect. A few low-cost ingredients and you have yourself several meals. You can even add a bit of rice to make it last longer.

1 Put all the ingredients in a slow cooker. Cover and cook on low for 8 hours. If you want to shorten the time, you can cook on high for about 4 hours. Once the soup is finished, remove the bay leaf.

2 Garnish with chopped parsley, if desired, and serve immediately or refrigerate for later. This soup should last at least 2 weeks in the fridge, or up to 6 months in the freezer.

Makes 8 to 9 servings

Prep and cook time: 4 hours 20 minutes to 8 hours 20 minutes

---

4 cups (960 ml) vegetable broth (see page 16)

3 cups (540 g) diced tomatoes (or one 28-ounce [794 g] can diced tomatoes, drained)

2 cups (345 g) cooked kidney beans (or one 15-ounce [425 g] can kidney beans, drained and rinsed)

2 cups (345 g) cooked pinto beans (or one 15-ounce [425 g] can pinto beans, drained and rinsed)

2 cups (360 g) cooked white beans (or one 15-ounce [425 g] can white beans, drained and rinsed)

4 carrots, peeled and sliced

4 celery stalks, diced

1 yellow onion, diced

1 bay leaf

1 tablespoon dried parsley

1 teaspoon salt (or to taste)

Chopped flat-leaf parsley for garnish, optional

TOMATO & CABBAGE SOUP

While many people may think of beet and cabbage borscht when cabbage soup comes to mind, tomatoes and cabbage go very well together, too. This is an inexpensive yet filling soup that can be thrown together in a few minutes and that will keep you satiated for quite a while. Plus cabbage is known to help lower cholesterol. Before you start, though, be aware this recipe makes a lot of soup. Beyond the vegetable broth and water, the cabbage and tomatoes both release a ton of liquid as well. I suggest making it over the weekend so you'll have lunch for the following week.

1 Combine all the ingredients in a large slow cooker. Cover and cook on high for 3 to 4 hours, until the cabbage is tender. If you want to cook it slower, you can put it on low for 8 hours. When it's done, remove the bay leaf.

2 Serve immediately or refrigerate for later. This soup will last about 2 weeks in the fridge or up to 6 months in the freezer.

Notes

Here's a time-saving tip: Freeze the soup in individual portions for quick meals on busy days.

Makes 6 to 7 servings

Prep and cook time: 4 hours 30 minutes to 8 hours 20 minutes

4 cups (960 ml) vegetable broth (see page 16)

3 cups (540 g) diced tomatoes (or one 28-ounce [794 g] can diced tomatoes, drained)

1 cup (240 ml) water

1 head green cabbage, cored, chopped

1 yellow onion, chopped

3 garlic cloves, minced

1 bay leaf

1 teaspoon salt (or to taste)

½ teaspoon ground black pepper

TOMATO BASIL SOUP

Tomato soup is a classic American dish. I used to love the Campbell's tomato soup in the can. With my whole food lifestyle, I obviously haven't had it in years, so I wanted to create a healthier, grown-up version. This soup is perfect for those busy days when you don't have any extra time to spend in the kitchen. The final product won't have an overly red look to it, but the flavor of the soup reminds me of being a kid. And since tomatoes are considered a heart-healthy food and are low in calories, this dish is a wonderful soup to start with if you're new to a whole food diet.

1 Put all the ingredients in a slow cooker. Cover and cook on high for at least 5 hours, up to 8 hours, until the vegetables have softened.

2 Once the soup is done, use an immersion blender to blend until smooth. If you don't have an immersion blender, you can transfer the soup to a standing blender and blend in batches.

3 This soup will last for at least a week in the fridge. You can also freeze it for up to 6 months.

Variation

If you want to make this soup creamy, you can add 1 cup (240 ml) coconut milk or almond milk right before you blend it.

Makes 4 servings

Prep and cook time: 5 to 8 hours

12 vine-ripened tomatoes, seeds removed

1 yellow onion, chopped

10 basil leaves

2 garlic cloves, minced

1 teaspoon salt (or to taste)

1 teaspoon dried oregano, optional

CORN CHOWDER

Who doesn't love the thick and creamy taste of corn chowder? The fat from coconut milk steps in to give this recipe the right consistency without the heavy cream and butter that traditional recipes call for. After cooking, the coconut flavor can't really be detected, either. The corn is the star of this recipe, and the hints of oregano and garlic add a flavor that will keep you coming back for more. This kid-friendly dish doesn't last long in my house. Plus, it's simple to make.

1 Put all the ingredients except the arrowroot and green onions in a large slow cooker and cover it. Turn the slow cooker to high and cook for 10 hours.

2 Remove the lid and stir in the arrowroot to thicken the soup.

3 Serve topped with green onions, if desired. This should last about 5 days in the fridge and up to 6 months in the freezer.

Makes 8 servings

Prep and cook time: 10 hours

4 cups (600 g) sweet corn kernels (see Notes)

3 cups (720 ml) vegetable broth (see page 16)

2½ cups (375 g) diced golden russet potatoes (about 1-inch [2.5 cm] cubes; see Notes)

1¾ cups (420 ml [one 13.5-ounce can]) full-fat coconut milk

2 tablespoons minced onion

1 to 2 teaspoons salt (or to taste)

1 teaspoon minced garlic (or 2 garlic cloves, minced)

1 teaspoon dried oregano

1 tablespoon arrowroot

Chopped green onions for garnish, optional

Variations

- Add ¼ cup (15 g) nutritional yeast for a cheesy flavor.

- You can also add 1 chopped jalapeño for the last hour of cooking for a kick.

Notes

- If you use frozen corn, you may need to adjust the amount of arrowroot powder to get the chowder to thicken a bit more.

- The recipe calls for golden russet potatoes for their buttery flavor, but red or Yukon Gold potatoes would be a good substitute. While you could use a plain russet potato, the other varieties do offer a bit of a different flavor.

- If you don't have 10 hours to let this simmer in a slow cooker, it also cooks well on the stove. Bring the ingredients to a boil in a large pot, then reduce the heat to medium-low, and let it simmer for 2 hours, covered. Add the arrowroot at the end if you need to thicken the soup.

LEMON & GARLIC ARTICHOKES

This simple recipe takes just a few minutes of prep time. More than a flavorful treat, artichoke hearts have liver-cleansing and cholesterol-lowering properties. This is perfect whether you're just eating the artichoke heart or using it in another dish.

1 The outer part of the artichoke can be quite fibrous and tough, so using a serrated knife, cut off the stem and about 1 inch (2.5 cm) off the top of each artichoke.

2 Starting with the outside leaves, gently pry open each artichoke, making room between the individual leaves. There are some small thorns on the end of each leaf, so be careful. Leave the bulb in the very middle intact (that's the artichoke heart).

3 Cut the lemon in half and, lightly squeezing, rub the top and bottom of each artichoke with half a lemon. This adds flavor and will keep the artichoke fresher as it cooks.

4 Brush 1 tablespoon olive oil on each artichoke, paying special attention to the heart in the middle of the artichoke.

5 Stick 2 or 3 garlic cloves into the middle of each artichoke. If you want it more garlicky, just add more cloves.

6 Place the vegetable broth and artichokes in the slow cooker and liberally apply the salt to the top of the artichokes. Cover and cook on high for 4 hours.

7 This dish should last about 1 week in the fridge (see Notes).

Makes 2 artichokes

Prep and cook time: 4 hours 20 minutes

2 artichokes

1 lemon

2 tablespoons olive oil

4 or 5 garlic cloves, peeled

1 cup (240 ml) vegetable stock (see page 16)

1 teaspoon salt (or to taste)

Notes

* To eat, simply remove each leaf and scrape your teeth along the bottom of the leaf. To gain access to the heart, remove the "fur" (or "choke") surrounding the inner part of the heart.

* The garlic in this recipe also becomes caramelized, and you can it eat whole. Yummy!

* This doesn't store well as an entire artichoke, so remove the leaves and scrape the good part out of the bottoms with a butter knife, then store with the hearts.

MARINATED MUSHROOMS

When I was a kid, I hated mushrooms. Now, as an adult, mushrooms are one of my favorite vegetables, especially when soaked in balsamic vinegar. Then again, pretty much anything is great with balsamic! Slow cooking these mushrooms allows the flavors to really develop. This recipe makes a small batch, so if you're feeding a crowd, you may want to double it. As a side dish, it pairs well with just about anything. You could even serve these mushrooms over quinoa for a complete meal.

1 Combine all the ingredients except the parsley in a slow cooker and turn it on high. Cover and cook for 3 to 6 hours. The longer the mushrooms cook, the more the flavors develop.

2 Garnish with chopped parsley, if desired, and serve immediately or refrigerate for later. This should last about 1 week in the fridge.

Makes 3 servings

Prep and cook time: 3 hours 10 minutes to 6 hours 10 minutes

1 pound (450 g) button or baby bella mushrooms, cleaned

½ cup (80 g) diced yellow onion

¼ cup (60 ml) balsamic vinegar

¼ cup (60 ml) water

2 tablespoons avocado oil (or olive oil)

1 teaspoon salt (or to taste)

½ teaspoon dried oregano

¼ teaspoon dried thyme

¼ cup (15 g) freshly chopped flat-leaf parsley, optional

CHILI MAC & CHEESE

Vegans don't need to go without mac and cheese! This chili version is comforting and cheesy without using any dairy. It's super-easy to make and can be done in the slow cooker while you're not even home. Much like the Corn Chowder (page 78), this is another recipe that will get picky eaters to switch to a healthier version of their favorite meals without having to sacrifice flavor. The green lentils add the texture of ground beef without the saturated fats, and all the ingredients together give it that classic chili flavor we love.

1 Combine all the ingredients except the macaroni and the Macadamia Nut Cheese Sauce in a large slow cooker. Cover, turn it on high, and cook for 3½ hours.

2 Add the macaroni and cook for 15 to 20 minutes, or until the pasta is done.

3 Pour in the cheese sauce and stir well.

4 Garnish with more paprika and chopped green onions, if desired, and serve immediately or refrigerate for later. This will keep in the fridge for at least a week. It can also be frozen for up to 6 months.

Variation

If you want some extra heat in this recipe, you can add ½ teaspoon cayenne or even some diced chile peppers.

Makes 9 to 10 servings

Prep and cook time: 4 hours

4 cups (960 ml) water

3 cups (540 g) diced tomatoes (or one 28-ounce [794 g] can diced tomatoes, drained)

2 cups (345 g) cooked pinto beans (or one 15-ounce [425 g] can pinto beans, drained and rinsed)

2 cups (320 g) diced yellow onion

1 cup (200 g) cooked green lentils

1½ teaspoons chili powder

1 teaspoon minced garlic (or 1 garlic clove, minced)

1 teaspoon salt (or to taste)

½ teaspoon smoked paprika, plus extra for garnish, optional

2 cups (210 g) uncooked brown rice elbow macaroni

2 cups (480 ml) Macadamia Nut Cheese Sauce (page 171)

Chopped green onion for garnish, optional

CHICKPEA CAULIFLOWER COCONUT CURRY

Curry powder is a great spice mix to work with. Although the exact ingredients may vary slightly, the mix typically features several superfoods. A yellow curry powder's main ingredients usually include turmeric, coriander, cumin, mustard seed, and either cardamom or cinnamon, if not both. I love curry for its health benefits and its deep, rich flavor. This dish is quite easy to make in a slow cooker, plus it tastes wonderful and is a great introduction for someone who doesn't quite yet have a palate for curry or Indian food in general.

1 Put all the ingredients except the kale in a slow cooker, cover, and cook on high for 5 hours.

2 Turn the heat off and add the kale. Stir, then cover for 20 minutes to cook the kale.

3 Uncover and serve. This will keep in the refrigerator for at least a week.

Notes

* For a bit of heat, you can add some red pepper flakes.

* This dish will be a little soupy, which is intended. It can be served by itself or on a bed of rice or quinoa. Use a slotted spoon if you don't want to get too much liquid on the plate while serving.

* To reheat this in the microwave, I suggest adding some extra water (about 1 tablespoon) so it doesn't dry out.

Makes 5 to 6 servings

Prep and cook time: 5 hours 35 minutes

4 cups (650 g) cooked chickpeas (or two 15-ounce [425 g] cans chickpeas, drained)

3 cups (300 g) chopped cauliflower (about 1 head cauliflower)

1½ cups (240 g) diced yellow onions

1 cup (100 g) snow peas

1¾ cups (420 ml) coconut milk (preferably full-fat)

1 cup (240 ml) vegetable broth (page 16)

2 teaspoons curry powder

2 teaspoons minced garlic

1 teaspoon garam masala

Salt to taste

4 or 5 kale leaves, chopped and massaged

CREAMY MUSHROOM RISOTTO

Risottos are classically made with veal, beef, or chicken stock and lots of butter. Clearly those aren't health-conscious, vegan-friendly choices. So to make a risotto that works for my family, I substitute with vegetable broth and just omit the butter, which isn't even really necessary.

1 Put everything in a slow cooker, cover, and cook on high for 3½ hours, stirring at least once. After 3 hours, check on the dish to be sure you don't overcook the rice.

2 Serve while it's still warm. Leftovers can be kept in the fridge for up to a week.

Variation

Parmesan cheese is a common risotto ingredient that's not friendly to vegans. If you want that cheesy flavor, you can add some nutritional yeast to the finished dish; anywhere from ¼ cup (15 g) to 1 cup (60 g) will work.

Note

Vegetables tend to release different amounts of liquid when they cook and can be a bit unpredictable, so the cooking time may vary slightly each time.

Makes 5 to 6 servings

Prep and cook time: 4 hours

3 cups (720 ml) vegetable broth (page 16)

2 cups (480 ml) almond milk

2 cups (320 g) diced onions

2 cups (320 g) green peas

2 cups (320 g) uncooked wild rice blend

8 ounces (225 g) mushrooms, chopped

8 ounces (225 g) mushrooms, thinly sliced

One 4-inch (10 cm) sprig fresh tarragon, chopped

1 teaspoon thyme

Salt to taste

BUTTERNUT SQUASH & WHITE BEAN CHILI

One of the most popular recipes on my blog is a sweet potato chili, which is where I got the inspiration to make this butternut squash and white bean version. If you can't find butternut squash, you can use sweet potatoes in its place. The white beans have a wonderful texture while adding some protein. The longer you let this sit in the slow cooker, the better it will taste.

1 Mix all the ingredients together in a slow cooker. Cover and cook on high for at least 8 hours. In my opinion, the longer it cooks, the better—I like to cook mine all day long.

2 Serve garnished with smoked paprika. Store the chili in an airtight container in the fridge. It should keep about 10 days. You can also freeze it for up to 6 months.

Notes

* If you plan on allowing this chili to cook all day, there's no need to cook the beans before using them in this recipe. Just soak 1½ cup dried beans in water overnight before using.

* If the chili seems a bit thin, add 2 tablespoons arrowroot to thicken it.

* If you want some heat in this chili, you can add 1 teaspoon cayenne.

Makes 6 to 7 servings

Prep and cook time: 8 hours 30 minutes

1 medium butternut squash, peeled and cubed

4 cups (960 ml) vegetable broth (see page 16)

3½ cups (630 g) diced tomatoes (or one 28-ounce [795 g] can diced tomatoes, drained)

3 cups (540 g) cooked white beans (or two 15-ounce [425 g] cans white beans, drained and rinsed) (see Notes)

1 onion, diced

2 or 3 garlic cloves, minced

1½ tablespoons chili powder

1½ teaspoons salt (or to taste)

1½ tablespoons smoked paprika, plus extra for garnish

HOMEMADE APPLESAUCE

pplesauce is very easy to make yourself. My great-grandmother made the best homemade applesauce; we all loved it as kids. Now every time I smell it cooking, I think of her. I hope she would be proud of my recipe. Slow cooking the apples brings out the natural sugars, so there's no need to add any. This can also double as a healthy pie filling! The longer you let it cook, the better it becomes. The recipe calls for at least 6 hours cooking, but you can leave it in the slow cooker for 8 or 9 hours with no issues. We often make this right before bedtime and wake up to a delicious-smelling kitchen.

1 Core and cut the apples into 1½-inch (4 cm) cubes. You can peel them or leave the skins on. (I leave the skins on to save time.)

2 Put all the ingredients in a slow cooker and mix well. Cover.

3 Turn the slow cooker on high and cook for at least 6 hours.

4 Once the apples are soft, you can use an immersion blender to purée them, or leave the applesauce chunky.

5 This applesauce will last a couple weeks in the fridge, or you can freeze it for up to 6 months.

Makes 3 cups (720 g)

Prep and cook time: 7 to 8 hours

---

10 to 12 apples (preferably Gala)

½ cup (120 ml) water

2 teaspoons ground cinnamon

1 teaspoon vanilla extract

¼ teaspoon ground cloves, optional

¼ teaspoon ground ginger

¼ teaspoon ground nutmeg

Notes

* If you plan on using the applesauce as a replacement for oil in baking, skip the spices and just cook the apples and water.

* One awesome thing you can do with this is make apple pie ice cream. In a blender, combine 2 cups (480 ml) full-fat coconut milk, 1 cup (240 ml) applesauce, and 2 to 3 tablespoons maple syrup. Pour into an ice cream machine and turn it on. It seriously tastes just like apple pie à la mode, but without the extra carbs!

BLACK BEAN & SWEET POTATO HASH

My husband and I both love sweet potatoes. Besides being tasty, they're a great source of vitamins, potassium, and carotenoids (the stuff, also in carrots, that's good for your eyes and immune system). The sweetness of the sweet potato combined with hearty black beans goes well with the smoked paprika and chili powder. Take care to man the fort while preparing this one. The sweet potatoes, if left unattended in the covered pan for too long, can turn to mush. I highly recommend adding avocado to get some healthy fats in the mix as well.

1 Add the avocado oil to a sauté pan on medium-high heat. Add the onion and pepper and cook until they are moderately soft, 5 to 7 minutes.

2 Reduce the heat to medium and add all the remaining ingredients except the avocado. Mix well, then cover. Cook, stirring occasionally, until everything is soft, 13 to 15 minutes.

3 Remove from the heat and serve immediately, topped with avocado slices, if desired, or refrigerate for later. This will last for about a week in the fridge.

Note

If you don't have black beans, pinto beans would be a perfectly good substitute, although this will alter the flavor a bit.

Makes 5 to 6 servings

Prep and cook time: 35 minutes

2 tablespoons avocado oil

½ cup (80 g) diced yellow onion

½ cup (40 g) diced red pepper (about ½ large red bell pepper)

4 cups (535 g) diced sweet potatoes (about 2 large sweet potatoes cut into ½-inch [1.25 cm] cubes)

1½ cups (255 g) cooked black beans (or one 15-ounce [425 g] can black beans, drained and rinsed)

2 teaspoons chili powder

2 teaspoons smoked paprika

½ teaspoon salt (or to taste)

Half an avocado, pitted, peeled, and sliced, optional

CREAMY ASPARAGUS SOUP

Asparagus was considered an aphrodisiac in ancient times; today it's known to aid in the transport of glucose through the bloodstream and to help remove carcinogens, making it an awesome cancer-fighting veggie. This soup can be prepped in about 10 minutes. All you need to do is let it simmer.

1 In a large stockpot, add the onion, garlic, and olive oil. Cook on medium heat until the onions start to soften, about 5 minutes.

2 While that's cooking, chop the asparagus into 1-inch (2.5 cm) pieces. You can reserve some of the tips for a nice garnish.

3 Add the vegetable broth, chopped asparagus, and salt to the stockpot. Turn on high and bring to a boil. Reduce the heat to medium-low and let the soup simmer for about 1 hour, covered.

4 Once everything has softened, use an immersion blender to purée the soup, then add most of the Basic Cashew Cream and purée until well combined.

5 Top with the remaining dollops of cashew cream and the asparagus tips, if using. Serve immediately or refrigerate for later. This should last at least 2 weeks in the fridge and up to 6 months in the freezer.

Makes 4 servings

Prep and cook time: 1 hour 30 minutes

1 large onion, diced

3 garlic cloves, chopped

2 tablespoons olive oil (see Variations)

2 bunches asparagus, trimmed

6 cups (1.4 L) vegetable broth (see page 16)

1 teaspoon salt (or to taste)

1 cup (240 ml) Basic Cashew Cream (page 175; see Variations)

Variations

* If you don't use oil, you can cook the onions and garlic in a little vegetable broth. To do this, pour a small amount of broth in the pan, about ¼ inch (6 mm) or less. Bring the broth to a low simmer on medium heat and add the vegetables. Turn the heat up slightly, taking care to move the vegetables around often so they don't burn. Once the liquid has evaporated, the vegetables should be done.

* If you have a nut allergy, you can use coconut cream instead of the cashew cream.

* If you want an extra fresh zing to this soup, add a little lemon juice at the very end, 1 teaspoon at a time to taste.

CARROT & APPLE SOUP

This carrot soup is a no-fuss dish that can be prepped in 15 to 20 minutes. The remaining time is simply a waiting game as it cooks on the stove. I love carrot soups for this very reason— it always seems I get a ton of flavor out of the soup without much effort. The apples and carrots provide a sweetness, while the garlic and onion remind you that this is a meal. Given its simplicity, if you're new to cooking or to healthier eating, this is a wonderful recipe to try. It's easy to make and the flavors are very enjoyable.

1 Place all the ingredients in a stockpot. Turn the stove to just above low heat, cover, and let simmer for an hour and half, until the vegetables and apples are softened.

2 Take off the lid and remove from the heat.

3 After the soup cools a bit, use an immersion blender to purée the ingredients together. If you don't have an immersion blender, you can use a standing blender, but be careful not to overfill it, and be sure the soup is not too hot when you transfer it to the blender. If the recipe needs a bit more salt, this a great time to add it.

4 Serve warm. Garnish with apple slices, if desired. This will keep in the refrigerator for 1 week, and in the freezer for up to 6 months.

Makes 5 to 6 servings

Prep and cook time: 1 hour 50 minutes

- 4 pounds (1.8 kg) carrots, peeled and chopped
- 6 Pink Lady apples (Gala would also work; see Notes), plus extra apple slices for garnish, optional
- 6 cups (1.4 L) vegetable broth (see page 16)
- 1 yellow onion, chopped
- 3 garlic cloves, chopped
- 1 to 2 teaspoon salt (or to taste)

Notes

- If you don't want this to be as sweet, simply remove an apple or two from the ingredients.

- This can be made in a slow cooker, too. Cook it on high for at least 4 hours, until the vegetables and apples are soft.

KALE & WILD RICE SALAD WITH TEMPEH

Tempeh is one of my favorite plant-based proteins. Like tofu, it's made from soybeans, but it differs in that it's made by fermenting cooked soybeans. It also has an earthier flavor than tofu, so it happens to pair nicely with the wild rice in this recipe. The baby kale provides an unexpected sweetness, and the ginger adds a little spice to make this dish truly memorable. I suggest cutting the tempeh into smaller pieces to allow it to be better coated with the sauce.

1 In a large saucepan, add the water and wild rice blend and bring to a boil. Reduce to a simmer, then cover and cook for about 40 minutes, until all the liquid is absorbed.

2 Add everything else except the kale and cook for 5 to 7 minutes.

3 Add the kale and mix until it's slightly wilted.

4 Serve immediately or refrigerate for later. This will last at least a week in the fridge.

Notes

* If you can't find mirin, check the Pantry section on page 12 for a good substitute.

* If you don't use oil, you can probably omit the toasted sesame oil, but I think it adds great flavor.

* If you avoid soy, you can use coconut aminos in place of the Bragg Liquid Aminos.

Makes 4 to 5 servings

Prep and cook time: 50 minutes

2 cups (480 ml) water

1 cup (160 g) uncooked wild rice blend

One 8-ounce (227 g) package tempeh

¼ cup (60 ml) apple cider vinegar

¼ cup (60 ml) mirin (see Notes)

2 tablespoons toasted sesame oil (see Notes)

1 tablespoon Bragg Liquid Aminos (see Notes)

2 teaspoons freshly minced ginger

1 teaspoon garlic powder (or 1 garlic clove, minced)

3 cups (50 g) baby kale or spinach, loosely packed

POMEGRANATE CHICKPEA SALAD

L ike many of the recipes I make, this is a great example of using simple ingredients and letting their flavors shine through. The onion and the pomegranate molasses mix well with the simplicity of the chickpeas—you won't be able to take just one bite. This recipe will quickly become a staple in your house, just as it is in ours, as an easy go-to when you're craving light, summery salad flavors.

1 Mix all the ingredients in a large bowl until everything is well incorporated. I used a spatula to mix it for about 1 minute.

2 Cover and place in the fridge for about 30 minutes to allow the flavors to marinate. The longer this sits, the better it gets. This salad should last at least 5 days in the fridge.

Notes

* Be sure to slice the red onion very thinly. If it's too thick, the onion flavor will overpower each bite. I use a mandoline to keep the onions a consistent thickness. If you can't slice them thin enough, use very small-diced red onions, almost minced.

* If you can't find pomegranate molasses, you can use balsamic vinegar in its place.

* If you want to play up the pomegranate flavor even more, add ½ cup (90 g) pomegranate seeds.

Makes 4 servings

Prep time: 40 minutes

4 cups (650 g) cooked chickpeas (or two 15-ounce [425 g] cans chickpeas, drained and rinsed)

½ cup (60 g) thinly sliced red onion (see Notes)

¼ cup (60 ml) orange juice (or the juice of 1 medium orange)

1 tablespoon pomegranate molasses (see Notes)

1 teaspoon salt (or to taste)

½ teaspoon ground cumin

¼ cup (15 g) freshly chopped flat-leaf parsley (or 2 teaspoons dried parsley)

1 teaspoon olive oil

SIMPLE CUCUMBER & DILL SALAD

Cucumber salads are a staple dish in spring and summer. The traditional cucumber salad this recipe seeks to replace is often bogged down with too much sugar, with some versions calling for as much as a cup of white sugar. Recipes like those stop being healthy, much as a taco salad loaded with beef, cheese, and sour cream in a deep-fried shell can't claim to be a salad anymore. This recipe calls for far less sugar, allowing the dill to be the star of the show. Easy to make with simple ingredients, this salad is a great addition to any meal.

1 Peel the cucumbers, if desired (I prefer to leave the skin on), then thinly slice them about ¼ inch (6 mm) thick. I suggest using a mandoline for this to make sure the slices are all the same thickness. Add the cucumbers to a large serving bowl with the dill and red onion.

2 In a small bowl, combine the water, vinegar, coconut sugar, and salt.

3 Pour the dressing over the cucumbers and mix well. Make sure all the cucumbers are evenly coated.

4 Cover and chill in the fridge for at least 1 hour. The flavors will get better the longer it sits. This salad should last at least 5 days in the fridge.

Makes 4 to 5 servings

Prep time: 1 hour 10 minutes

2 large cucumbers, trimmed

¼ cup (8 g) freshly chopped dill

¼ cup (30 g) thinly sliced red onion

3 tablespoons water

3 tablespoons white wine vinegar

1½ tablespoons coconut sugar

¼ teaspoon salt (or to taste)

BROCCOLI SALAD

Broccoli salad is a staple at many summer parties. Traditionally it comes with a mayonnaise base and is topped with bacon. To make this vegan, I started with my cashew cream for the base. I substituted pepitas (pumpkin seeds) for the crunch and fat factor in lieu of bacon. The cranberries add that hint of sweetness and are an interesting twist from the more traditional apples. This salad gets better the longer it sits, so I highly recommend making it at least 30 minutes before you plan to eat it. If refrigerating overnight, mix in ½ teaspoon water before serving to help the cashew cream reconstitute a bit.

1 Mix together all the salad ingredients in a large bowl and toss well.

2 In a small bowl, mix together the dressing ingredients and stir well.

3 Pour the dressing over the salad ingredients and mix until everything is evenly coated, for about 1 minute.

4 Serve immediately or refrigerate for later. This should keep in the fridge for at least a week.

Variations

* Feel free to use sunflower seeds or any nut you like in place of the pepitas. I think pecans would work nicely here as well.

* Those with nut allergies can use a vegan plain yogurt as a base instead of the cashew cream.

Makes 4 servings

Prep time: 20 minutes

SALAD

2 large heads broccoli, cut into florets (or 5 cups [450 g] broccoli florets)

1 large carrot, peeled and shredded (or 1½ cups [165 g] shredded carrots)

1 cup (120 g) dried cranberries

½ cup (60 g) pepitas (pumpkin seeds; see Variations)

¼ cup (30 g) thinly sliced red onion

DRESSING

½ cup (120 ml) Basic Cashew Cream (page 175; see Variations)

1 tablespoon apple cider vinegar

1 tablespoon maple syrup

½ teaspoon salt (or to taste)

WILD RICE WITH MUSHROOMS & SPINACH

Wild rice is a great base in recipes. It adds that classic earthy, nutty flavor while extending the number of meals you can get out of your efforts in the kitchen. The spinach and mushrooms go well with the wild rice in this dish. The white wine vinegar really adds the special touch that makes it all worth your time, too. We've eaten this cold and warm, and both ways work, although I prefer eating it warm.

1 In a saucepan, bring the vegetable broth and wild rice blend to a boil. Lower to a simmer and cook until all the broth is absorbed, about 40 minutes.

2 In another saucepan, combine the oil, garlic, onion, and white wine vinegar on medium-high heat and cook for 6 to 8 minutes, until the onions begin to soften.

3 Add the mushrooms and stir for another 5 minutes or so, until softened.

4 Once the rice is done, add it to the saucepan with the mushroom and onion mixture.

5 Add salt and pepper, then mix in the spinach. Cook until the spinach is slightly wilted, 2 to 3 minutes.

6 Remove the dish from the heat and serve immediately or refrigerate for later. This should last at least 4 days in the fridge. You can also freeze it for up to 6 months.

Makes 4 to 5 servings

Prep and cook time: 45 minutes

---

3 cups (720 ml) vegetable broth (see page 16)

1½ cups (240 g) uncooked wild rice blend

1 tablespoon avocado oil

1 garlic clove, minced

½ yellow onion, chopped

2 tablespoons white wine vinegar

8 ounces (225 g) mushrooms, thinly sliced

Salt and pepper to taste

3 to 4 cups (55 to 75 g) loosely packed baby spinach

LENTIL SHEPHERD'S PIE

Shepherd's pie is a traditional comfort food. I know I had my share as a child. Made with ground beef and white potatoes, the conventional version can hardly be considered a healthy meal. To make mine vegan, I use lentils in place of the ground beef, and instead of white potatoes, I use a cauliflower mash. Both these substitutions make for a far healthier alternative. The results are so good, we've been known to eat this out of the serving dish.

1 Place all the ingredients for the lentil mixture in an ovenproof 9-inch (23 cm) sauté pan (see Note). Cover and cook on medium to low heat, simmering for 30 minutes.

2 Preheat the oven to 350°F (180°C).

3 While the lentil mixture is simmering, add all the ingredients for the cauliflower mash to a food processor and blend until smooth, 1 to 2 minutes.

4 Once the lentil mixture is cooked through and all the water has been absorbed, add the cauliflower mash on top.

5 Place the pan in the oven and bake for 45 minutes. You can tell it's done when the cauliflower mash is golden brown around the edges.

6 Garnish with parsely, if desired, and serve or refrigerate for later. This should last at least a week in the fridge. It also freezes for up to 6 months.

Note

If you don't have an ovenproof pan, cook this in a regular pan and transfer to a 9 × 13-inch (23 × 33 cm) baking dish.

Makes 5 to 6 servings

Prep and cook time: 1 hour 15 minutes

LENTIL MIXTURE

2 cups (320 g) diced onion (or 1 onion, diced)

2 cups (480 ml) vegetable broth (see page 16)

1 cup (200 g) cooked green or brown lentils

1 cup (150 g) sweet corn kernels

1 cup (160 g) green peas

1 teaspoon dried parsley

½ teaspoon dried sage

½ teaspoon salt (or to taste)

CAULIFLOWER MASH

1 head cauliflower, cut into florets

1½ cups (360 ml) coconut milk (or one 13.5-ounce [400 ml] can full-fat coconut milk)

1 garlic clove, minced

½ teaspoon salt (or to taste)

Chopped flat-leaf parsely for garnish, optional

EGGPLANT & CHICKPEAS WITH TOMATOES

This classic Mediterranean dish is perfect to make when you're busy with other things. The whole process takes 45 minutes, but most of that time is spent letting the dish stew on the stove or waiting for the eggplant to drain its excess moisture. If you've never used eggplant, this is a great place to start. An extremely versatile vegetable, it's sort of like a natural tofu, with a mild taste that likes to soak up any flavor you cook it with. It's also considered "brain food" and helps lower LDL (often referred to as "bad cholesterol").

1 Place the eggplant in a colander. Salt the eggplant and let it sit in the colander for at least 15 minutes. This removes some of the bitterness and also draws out liquid. Don't skip this step.

2 After about 10 minutes into salting the eggplant, place the tomato, onions, and vegetable broth in a large pan on medium to medium-low heat and begin to soften the onion.

3 Place the eggplant and remaining ingredients in the pan, reduce the heat to low, and cover. Cook for approximately 30 minutes, stirring occasionally.

4 Serve immediately or refrigerate for later. This should last at least a week in the fridge. I don't recommend freezing it.

Makes 4 servings

Prep and cook time: 45 minutes

1 medium eggplant, diced

1 teaspoon salt (or to taste) plus extra for salting eggplant

3 cups (540 g) chopped tomatoes

2 cups (320 g) chopped onions (about 1 large yellow onion)

¼ cup (60 ml) vegetable broth (see page 16)

1 teaspoon minced garlic (about 1 garlic clove)

3 cups (500 g) cooked chickpeas (or two 15-ounce [425 g] cans chickpeas, drained and rinsed)

½ teaspoon ground cumin

½ teaspoon ground turmeric

VEGGIE-LOADED STIR-FRY

Stir-fries are a great way to off-load whatever vegetables are sitting around the house. As a twist, I use cauliflower rice as a substitute for the grain. This dish is packed with nutrients from the peppers, cauliflower, broccoli, and more. Moreover, because it uses coconut aminos, it's soy-free. One thing that stands out to me about this dish is how beautiful it looks. If you're looking to "eat the rainbow," this is a great place to start.

1 Remove the stem from the cauliflower and roughly chop the florets. Place them in a food processor and pulse a few times until the cauliflower takes on a rice-like consistency.

2 Add 1 tablespoon of the toasted sesame oil to a pan on medium heat. Add the cauliflower rice and sauté for 5 to 6 minutes, or until the rice starts to look slightly toasted. Set aside.

3 In the same pan, add the remaining 1 tablespoon toasted sesame oil, along with the ginger and garlic. Sauté for 1 to 2 minutes. Add the carrots, peppers, broccoli, and green peas. Sauté for another minute.

4 Add the cauliflower rice, coconut aminos, lime juice, and salt. Sauté for a minute and then cover. Cook just long enough for the broccoli to soften a bit, about 2 minutes.

5 Garnish with the green onions and serve immediately. This should last for about a week in the fridge. I don't recommend freezing it.

Makes 4 servings

Prep and cook time: 40 minutes

1 head cauliflower

2 tablespoons toasted sesame oil

½ to 1 tablespoon minced ginger (or to taste)

2 garlic cloves, minced

2 carrots, shredded

1 red bell pepper, thinly sliced

1 yellow bell pepper, thinly sliced

1 head broccoli, cut into florets and chopped

1 cup (160 g) green peas

¼ cup (60 ml) coconut aminos

Juice of 1 lime

1 teaspoon salt (or to taste)

2 green onions, chopped

Variations

If you want to add protein to this, add some baked tofu or about 1 cup (140 g) toasted cashews:

- To bake tofu, preheat the oven to 350°F (180°C). Drain a block of firm tofu and pat it dry, then cube it and place on a lined baking sheet. Brush with sesame oil and sprinkle with a little salt. Bake for 35 minutes, until the edges are golden.

- To toast cashews, preheat the oven to 400°F (200°C) and bake on a baking sheet for 5 to 10 minutes, turning once, until lightly browned. Watch them closely after the first 5 minutes to make sure they don't burn.

ROASTED RED PEPPER ZUCCHINI PASTA

Spiralizing zucchini is a great alternative for those trying to reduce their grain intake. It can take a heavy pasta dish and turn it into an enjoyable meal that doesn't leave you feeling bloated. This dish is all about the sauce, and while it might seem like a lot of work, it makes a lot of sauce. To save time, you can buy the roasted red peppers and roasted tomatoes in most grocery stores.

1 Preheat the oven to 350°F (180°C). Line a baking sheet with parchment paper.

2 Core the tomatoes and remove the insides of the bell peppers. Slice the peppers in half and place them on the baking sheet. Place the tomatoes on the baking sheet whole. Brush the tomatoes and peppers with 2 tablespoons of the avocado oil. Roast for 40 to 45 minutes.

3 Fill a large bowl with ice water. When the tomatoes are done roasting, place them into the ice bath. This will make it easy to peel the skins without burning your fingers.

4 Once the tomatoes are peeled, put them and the peppers in a large stockpot with the chili powder, salt, onion powder, smoked paprika, coriander, and cumin. Use an immersion blender to blend the sauce until smooth. If you don't have an immersion blender, you can transfer to a standing blender and purée in batches. Set aside.

5 Using a spiralizer, slice each zucchini into pasta. If you don't have a spiralizer, you can use a julienne peeler to make the pasta.

6 Place the zucchini in a large sauté pan with the remaining 1 teaspoon avocado oil. Quickly sauté on medium heat for about 1 minute, just long enough to warm up the pasta a little.

7 Pour the sauce over the pasta and serve immediately. If you plan to refrigerate for later, you should keep the sauce and pasta separate, as the zucchini pasta might release water once it's stored.

Makes 6 to 7 servings

Prep and cook time: 50 minutes

9 vine-ripened tomatoes

5 large red bell peppers

2 tablespoons plus 1 teaspoon avocado oil

1 teaspoon chili powder

1 teaspoon salt (or to taste)

½ teaspoon onion powder

½ teaspoon smoked paprika

¼ teaspoon ground coriander

¼ teaspoon ground cumin

3 medium zucchini

Note

This recipe makes a lot of sauce. If you have some left over, it freezes great. It should last up to 6 months in the freezer. I like to freeze this in serving-size containers so I only need to pull out what I need.

OATMEAL SNACK BARS

A decent healthy snack can be hard to come by these days. I'm always looking for healthy snack foods that are good on the go. These oatmeal snack bars fit the bill—and no baking required! They taste amazing, travel well, and provide the needed pick-me-up without the crash. Not only are these snack bars easy to make, but they're packed with protein and fiber that will keep you full until you get home from a busy day.

1. In a food processor, pulse the oats and cinnamon a few times.

2. Add the remaining ingredients except the water and raisins. Blend until the mixture comes together, 1 to 2 minutes. If it seems dry, add a little bit of water at a time until it is the consistency of peanut butter. You just want the dough to hold together, so don't make it too wet.

3. Add the raisins and pulse a few times to get them evenly dispersed.

4. Line an 8 x 8-inch (20 x 20 cm) glass baking dish with parchment paper. Make sure you leave a little paper sticking out of the sides of the dish. This will make the bars easier to remove once chilled.

5. Using a spatula, spoon the mixture into the lined baking dish. The dough will be pretty sticky, so wetting the spatula helps. Press the mixture down using the sides of the parchment paper.

6. Place the dish in the fridge to chill and firm up about 30 minutes.

7. Once the mixture is firm, use the ends of the parchment paper to pull it out of the pan. Cut into bars with a pizza cutter. These bars should be stored in the fridge in an airtight container. They will last about 2 weeks. You can also freeze them for up to 6 months.

Makes 9 large squares or 16 small squares

Prep and chill time: 35 minutes

---

2 cups (190 g) gluten-free rolled oats (see Variations)

1 teaspoon ground cinnamon

1¼ cups (340 g) unsalted peanut butter (see Variations)

½ cup (120 ml) maple syrup (see Variations)

¼ cup (30 g) pepitas (pumpkin seeds) or sunflower seeds

½ teaspoon salt

2 tablespoons water (if needed)

⅓ cup (50 g) raisins

Variations

- For a grain-free option, use quinoa flakes in place of the gluten-free rolled oats.

- To make these nut-free, use sunflower butter in place of the peanut butter.

- If you are using a salted peanut butter, omit the salt.

- If you would like to cut down the amount of maple syrup, you can use applesauce in place of half the maple syrup.

HEALTHY TRAIL MIX

Makes 5 cups (750 g)

Prep and cook time: 35 minutes

We're an on-the-go family, so I make sure to carry lots of snacks to keep us satiated. This trail mix is perfect for road trips, picnics, and long days running errands. It doesn't need refrigeration and provides you with healthy fat, protein, and some carbs to keep you going. You can use it as a base and add in whatever flavors you like—the combinations are endless.

1 Preheat the oven to 350°F (180°C). Line a baking sheet with parchment paper.

2 In a large bowl, mix together the almonds, apricots, cashews, pumpkin seeds, dates, cinnamon, and ground vanilla beans. Stir until everything looks well mixed.

3 Add the maple syrup and stir until everything is evenly covered, about 1 minute.

4 Spread the mixture on the baking sheet and sprinkle the salt on top.

5 Bake for 20 minutes, stopping halfway through to shake the pan.

6 It's important to let this cool completely, which could take a couple hours. Store the trail mix in an airtight container in the pantry. It should keep for several weeks. You can also freeze it for up to 6 months.

1½ cups (210 g) raw almonds

1 cup (180 g) chopped dried apricots

1 cup (140 g) raw cashew pieces

1 cup (120 g) pepitas (pumpkin seeds) or sunflower seeds

½ cup (90 g) Medjool dates, pitted and chopped

1 teaspoon ground cinnamon

1 teaspoon ground vanilla beans

⅓ cup (80 ml) maple syrup

½ teaspoon salt

Variations

* The fruit and nuts are substitutable, so feel free to use what you have on hand.

* Unsweetened shredded coconut would go nicely in here. Start with ½ cup (30 g).

Notes

* If the mixture starts to clump together after baking and cooling, just break it up with your hands.

* I would avoid adding chocolate chips if you plan on taking this in the car. They tend to melt and can be quite messy. If you do add them, wait for the mixture to cool, and store it in a cool location.

CINNAMON BANANA CHIPS

Makes 50 to 60 banana chips
Prep and cook time: 23 hours

2 bananas, thinly sliced

1 teaspoon ground cinnamon

½ teaspoon salt, optional

Making fruit chips or fruit leathers can take a bit of time, but it's much cheaper than buying store-bought versions. Plus, you can make a variety of flavors that you probably won't find in the stores. Don't let the long prep and cook time scare you—it's really very easy; it just takes a while to dry the chips. The key is cooking them at a very low temperature to preserve as many nutrients as possible. A dehydrator takes very little energy to run, and it won't heat up your house like the oven would. Much like a slow cooker, a dehydrator can run without you being home. My kids love these chips and they often don't even make it into a storage container!

1 Line your dehydrator trays with parchment paper. Place the banana slices on top of the parchment and sprinkle with cinnamon and the salt, if using.

2 Turn on the dehydrator and set it to 135°F (57°C). Dry for 23 hours, or until the chips are completely dried and easy to remove from the paper. If the chips still stick to the paper, they're not quite done yet.

3 Store the chips in a glass jar with rice scattered on the bottom to absorb extra moisture. They should keep in the pantry for several weeks.

Note

If you don't have a dehydrator, you can make these in the oven. Bake them for at least 8 hours in a 215°F (100°C) oven.

CHOCOLATE RASPBERRY BROWNIES

The flavors of coffee, chocolate, and raspberry work so well together, especially in this easy brownie recipe. They're quick to make, with little cleanup, and are irresistible. Substitute the raspberries with other berries, if you like.

1 Preheat the oven to 350°F (180°C). Line an 8 x 8-inch (20 x 20 cm) glass baking dish with parchment paper. Make sure you leave some parchment paper sticking out of the sides. This will make the whole thing easier to lift out once it's cooked.

2 In a medium bowl, mix all the dry ingredients.

3 In a large bowl, mix all the wet ingredients except the jam.

4 Add the dry ingredients to the wet and mix only until combined, using a hand mixer or a spatula.

5 Gently fold the raspberry jam into the batter.

6 Spoon the batter into the baking dish.

7 Bake for about 25 minutes, until a toothpick comes out clean.

8 Let the brownies cool completely, about 30 minutes, before removing them from the dish and cutting into bars. I use a pizza cutter to cut mine.

9 Keep these brownies stored in the fridge, where they should last a couple weeks. You can also freeze them for up to 6 months.

Makes 18 brownies

Prep and cook time: 35 minutes

2 cups (210 g) gluten-free oat flour

1 cup (90 g) cocoa powder or ¾ cup (80 g) cacao powder (see Variations)

1 teaspoon baking powder

½ teaspoon salt

2 flax eggs (see page 10)

½ cup (120 ml) maple syrup

¼ cup (60 ml) almond milk

¼ cup (60 g) applesauce (see page 7)

¼ cup (60 ml) melted coconut oil (see Variations)

1 teaspoon coffee extract (see Variations)

1 teaspoon vanilla extract

¾ cup (180 ml) Raspberry Vanilla Chia Jam (page 178)

Variations

- If you prefer to use cacao powder instead of cocoa powder, make sure to reduce the amount. Also keep in mind that the cacao will make the brownies taste a little bitter.

- If you avoid oil, you can replace the coconut oil with more applesauce. If you do that, you need to grease the parchment paper so the brownies don't stick.

- If you can't find coffee extract, you can use instant coffee granules (see pages 10–11) or omit altogether.

- Another great addition to this might be ½ cup (90 g) chocolate chips for an extra chocolate punch.

CREAMY ORANGE POPS

My kids love ice pops, but I refuse to buy most store-bought brands, since they're laden with food dyes, are high in sugar, and lack real nutritional value. You can easily make your own pops much more cheaply, and they'll be much more nutritious. I'm a firm believer that kids can't turn down anything in pop form, so this is a great opportunity to sneak some veggies in. Two vegetables you can easily sneak into these pops are carrots and sweet potatoes. Since they're the same orange color, they'll go virtually undetected! I suggest adding 1 large carrot, chopped, or ½ cup (70 g) raw chopped sweet potato.

Makes 8 ice pops

Prep and chill time: 6 hours 5 minutes

One 13.5-ounce (400 ml) can full-fat coconut milk

1 large navel orange, peeled and sliced

2 to 3 tablespoons maple syrup

1 Place all the ingredients in a blender and blend until smooth.

2 Pour into ice pop molds and place in the freezer to firm up. It will take about 6 hours.

3 Enjoy! These should last in the freezer for up to 6 months.

Note

When you're ready to eat a pop, just run the mold under hot water for a few seconds to loosen the mold.

MINI BLUEBERRY CHEESECAKES

ashews are an amazing ingredient. They can mimic so many non-vegan ingredients that they've become a staple in my kitchen despite their expense. If you want to enjoy cheesecake as a vegan, more than likely you'll eat something with a cashew base. This blueberry cheesecake is so rich and decadent, you'll forget there isn't any actual cream cheese or other form of dairy in it. The blueberries will melt in your mouth and keep you coming back for more. The best part of this recipe is its versatility—any type of berry, from strawberries to blackberries, would work great.

1 In a food processor, combine the almonds and dates. Slowly add the water, 1 teaspoon at a time as needed, until the mixture clumps together.

2 Place liners in a muffin pan (I used standard-size muffin cups with silicone liners). Press a little bit of crust into each muffin cup. Place in the fridge while you make the cheesecake filling.

3 In a food processor, combine the cheesecake ingredients until the mixture is smooth, 1 to 2 minutes.

4 Spoon the cheesecake mixture into each muffin cup, filling it all the way to the top. Once all the muffin cups are filled, place the muffin pan into the fridge to firm up. It will take a good 6 hours until completely firm. You can also put the cheesecakes into the freezer for about 1½ hours to speed up the process.

5 Serve topped with fresh blueberries, if desired. These can be kept in the fridge or the freezer. They should last about 2 weeks in the fridge and up to 6 months in the freezer.

Makes 18 mini cheesecakes

Prep and cook time: 6 hours 15 minutes

CRUST

1½ cups (210 g) raw almonds

8 to 10 Medjool dates, pitted

1 to 2 teaspoons water

CHEESECAKE

2 cups (280 g) raw cashews, soaked in water overnight

1½ cups (225 g) fresh blueberries (or frozen blueberries, thawed), plus more for optional topping

½ cup (120 ml) maple syrup

⅓ cup (80 ml) melted coconut oil

Juice of 1 lemon (or 2 tablespoons lemon juice)

½ teaspoon salt

Variations

* If you want to make one big cheesecake instead of the mini cheesecakes, you can use a 6-inch (15 cm) springform pan.

* As mentioned, any berry can be used in place of the blueberries.

PEANUT BUTTER CHOCOLATE CHIP QUINOA BARS

D on't let the quinoa scare you away from these delicious bars. Quinoa flakes are very similar to quick oats in texture, and they can be used interchangeably. This dish requires few ingredients and is easily adapted by adding in your own favorites, such as seeds or dried fruit. The quinoa flakes give these bars a nutty taste and texture that go very well with the peanut butter and chocolate. Then again, doesn't everything taste better with chocolate?

1 Combine all the ingredients except the chocolate chips in a food processor for 1 to 2 minutes.

2 Once everything looks well combined, add ⅓ cup chocolate chips and pulse a few times to mix them in.

3 Line an 8 x 8-inch (20 x 20 cm) baking dish with parchment paper. Leave enough paper to stick out of the sides to make it easy to lift the entire thing out at once.

4 Using your palms, press the mixture down into the baking dish. Make sure you press down very well to ensure everything sticks together.

5 Press the remaining 2 tablespoons chocolate chips on the top of the mixture.

6 Place the baking dish in the fridge for about 30 minutes to firm up.

7 Once it's firm, use a knife or pizza cutter to cut into squares.

8 These bars need to be kept in the fridge, where they should last up to 2 weeks. You can also freeze them for up to 6 months. If you decide to freeze them, I highly suggest wrapping them individually in plastic wrap before placing in the freezer.

Makes 9 large squares or 16 small squares

Prep and chill time: 35 minutes

2 cups (210 g) quinoa flakes (see Variations)

1½ cups (405 g) unsalted peanut butter (see Variations)

½ cup (120 ml) maple syrup (see Variations)

½ teaspoon salt

⅓ cup (60 g) chocolate chips plus 2 tablespoons for sprinkling on top

Variations

• You can use gluten-free quick oats in place of the quinoa flakes if you want.

• If you have a nut allergy, you can use sunflower butter in place of the peanut butter.

ENTERTAIN:
Favorites for a Crowd

Sure, we all splurge from time to time—there's no better time to splurge than when having guests over. A point of constant stress when entertaining is, of course, what kinds of food to serve. Whether you're having a dinner party or just want to put out some hors d'oeuvre for friends dropping by, these recipes are fun, healthy twists on classic party food. There's no reason to ditch your healthy lifestyle when you're having guests over for a meal. Recipes such as the Stuffed Sweet Potato Skins, Stuffed Peppers, and Three-Ingredient No-Bake Almond Butter Cookies are sure to please.

CINNAMON ROLL MUFFINS

Despite how awesome traditional cinnamon rolls are, they can be quite time-consuming to make from scratch as well as loaded with sugar, and they don't exactly inspire thoughts of healthy eating. I wanted to create a muffin recipe that would provide all the flavor of a cinnamon roll—the sweet bread, the unmistakable taste of cinnamon, the gooeyness in each bite—without sacrificing health. The other nice thing about these? They aren't nearly as messy to make or to eat. You won't feel like you need give your kids a bath after they're done eating. These are fun to make and share with family and friends. I hope you enjoy them as much as we do!

1 Preheat the oven to 350°F (180°C). Prepare the muffin pans: I use silicone liners so there's no need to grease them. If you use paper liners, you will need to grease them before you add the muffin mixture (if you don't, the muffins will stick to the paper). You can also skip the liners altogether and just grease the muffin pans.

2 Drain the dates and place them in a small blender or food processor along with ½ teaspoon of the cinnamon. Blend until you get a syrupy consistency. You may need to add a little water if the mixture seems thick. Start with ½ teaspoon at a time. Set aside.

3 In a large bowl, add the remaining teaspoon of cinnamon and the other dry ingredients. Stir quickly. Add the applesauce, maple syrup, almond milk, and vanilla extract to the bowl with the dry ingredients and combine. Mix in the flax eggs.

4 Once the ingredients in the bowl are all mixed, slowly fold in the cinnamon-date syrup. Don't mix it in entirely; just lightly swirl it in with a spatula.

5 Using a large cookie scoop or spoon, place the batter into lined muffin pans.

6 Bake for 10 to 12 minutes, until a toothpick comes out clean. Let the muffins cool completely before removing them from the muffin pans (about 20 minutes).

7 Serve immediately or refrigerate for later. They should last a couple of weeks in the fridge. You can also freeze them for up to 6 months.

Makes 12 standard-size muffins

Prep and cook time: 45 minutes

---

8 Medjool dates, pitted and soaked in water for at least 30 minutes

1½ teaspoons ground cinnamon

2 cups (210 g) gluten-free oat flour

1 teaspoon baking powder

1 teaspoon baking soda

½ teaspoon salt

½ cup (120 g) applesauce (see page 7)

¼ cup (60 ml) maple syrup

2 tablespoons almond milk

1 teaspoon vanilla extract

2 flax eggs (see page 10)

SALTED CARAMEL OVERNIGHT OATS

When I first began eating a whole food vegan diet, I never thought caramel would be something I would enjoy again. Discovering how to make a vegan salted caramel sauce changed that. This healthy breakfast tastes like a dessert but with less guilt. When I make overnight oats for myself, I like to make four servings at a time so I have breakfast for the week. But this breakfast is also easy enough to prepare for guests; just double the recipe. This way breakfast requires no cooking or preparation, which is great when we're all in a hurry in the morning or when out-of-town guests are visiting. The oats are made in jars, so they travel well to work; you can eat them hot or cold, whatever your preference. Overnight oats are extremely versatile, simple, and one of my favorites.

1 Mix all the ingredients in a large bowl and stir well.

2 Either leave in the bowl or spoon into separate 8-ounce jars. Cover and place in the fridge overnight.

3 You can eat this hot or cold. If you want to warm it up, put a portion in the microwave for 30 seconds, or warm it in a saucepan on medium-low heat for a few minutes.

Makes 4 servings

Prep time: 10 minutes

2½ cups (600 ml) almond milk (see Variations)

2 cups (350 g) gluten-free steel-cut oats or 2 cups (190 g) gluten-free rolled oats (see Variations)

¼ cup (60 ml) Salted Caramel Sauce (page 182)

2 Medjool dates, pitted and chopped (or 1 teaspoon maple syrup)

1 tablespoon plus 1 teaspoon chia seeds

1 tablespoon plus 1 teaspoon hemp hearts

2 teaspoons ground vanilla beans

Variations

• If you have a nut allergy, any dairy-free milk will work.

• I like to use gluten-free steel-cut oats for this because the steel-cut oats retain a crunch. If you prefer a smoother oatmeal, you can use gluten-free rolled oats.

• Feel free to add other ingredients—this recipe is very adaptable. A couple teaspoons of shredded coconut on top would work nicely with these flavors. You can also add a couple teaspoons of flaxseed meal for extra healthy good fats.

BLACK BEAN & CORN BREAKFAST BURRITOS

Sweet breakfasts don't always hit the spot . . . sometimes you just need a good savory breakfast to fill up your tank in the morning. This recipe should do the trick. The classic south-of-the-border black bean and corn combination goes great with some avocado and a bit of fresh cilantro on top—and it makes a nice presentation when serving guests. If you're looking to increase your vegetable intake, look no further. This recipe contains a decent variety of vegetables, so dig in and enjoy.

1 Put the tomatoes, water, onion, rice, and oil in large sauté pan on medium-low heat. Cover and cook for about 40 minutes. You'll need to check on this periodically to make sure the water doesn't all get absorbed too soon. If the water gets too low and the rice isn't done cooking, add more water—¼ cup (60 ml) at a time—until the rice is cooked. If it finishes before 40 minutes, continue to the next step.

2 Stir in the rest of the ingredients except the tortillas, cover, and cook for about 5 minutes on medium heat.

3 Remove from the heat, then place the filling in the tortillas. Wrap them up into burritos and serve. These should last in the fridge for at least a week.

Variations

* Get creative with your burritos by adding sliced avocado, cilantro, salsa, dairy-free sour cream, and/or lime juice.

* For a lower-carb option, wrap the filling in lettuce or serve on a bed of greens such as spinach, arugula, and baby kale.

Note

If you want to freeze these, wrap the burritos in plastic wrap first. Then you can just grab and reheat when you want them. You can also freeze the filling by itself. Frozen, these should last for up to 6 months.

Makes 4 burritos

Prep and cook time: 45 minutes

2 cups (360 g) diced tomatoes (about 4 tomatoes)

1½ cups (360 ml) water

1 cup (160 g) diced yellow onion (about 1 small onion)

½ cup (80 g) uncooked wild rice blend

1 tablespoon avocado oil

2 cups (345 g) cooked black beans (or one 15-ounce [425 g] can black beans, drained and rinsed)

1 cup (150 g) sweet corn kernels

½ cup (75 g) diced green pepper (about 1 green bell pepper)

1½ teaspoons salt (or to taste)

¾ teaspoon ground cumin

1 garlic clove, minced

4 large gluten-free tortillas

LEMON GARLIC ZUCCHINI STICKS

Zucchini is one of those vegetables that can go into just about any kind of recipe. While the combinations are endless for such a versatile vegetable, pairing it with lemon and garlic will keep your taste buds singing. It doesn't hurt that zucchini is low in calories, with only 17 calories per 100 grams. It's also high in antioxidants, and the skins are high in fiber. This is a healthy, tasty treat you can feel good about feeding to your family, especially since these zucchini sticks aren't fried or dipped in bread crumbs, as in more traditional recipes.

Makes 24 zucchini sticks

Prep and cook time: 45 minutes

- 3 medium to large zucchini
- ⅓ cup (80 ml) lemon juice
- 1 tablespoon olive oil
- ½ teaspoon minced garlic
- ¼ teaspoon dried basil
- ¼ teaspoon onion powder
- ¼ teaspoon salt (or to taste)
- 2 tablespoons nutritional yeast (see Notes)

1. Preheat the oven to 375°F (190°C). Line a baking sheet with parchment paper.

2. Cut the ends off the zucchini, then slice the zucchini widthwise down the middle, leaving you with two pieces half the length of the original zucchini. Quarter each half lengthwise and place on the baking sheet.

3. In a small bowl, mix the lemon juice, olive oil, garlic, dried basil, onion powder, and salt. Using a silicone brush, brush the mixture onto the zucchini.

4. Using your fingers, dust each zucchini stick with a little nutritional yeast, covering it completely.

5. Bake the zucchini sticks for 40 minutes. They will be lightly golden brown when done.

6. Remove from the oven and let cool slightly before serving. These should last 1 week in the fridge.

Notes

- These will not turn out super-crispy, as there isn't any breading on them and they're not pan-seared or fried. If you want to make them crispy, turn your oven to broil for the last 2 to 3 minutes of cooking.

- You can add a bit more nutritional yeast if you want a stronger cheese flavor.

- You might have some leftover lemon garlic sauce at the end; I find sauces like this can double as salad dressing.

STUFFED SWEET POTATO SKINS

Stuffed potato skins are an all-American favorite, but when made in the traditional style, they're far from healthy. They normally come loaded with cheese, bacon, and sour cream. I wanted to show that with a little ingenuity, even some of the unhealthiest dishes can be reinvented. This healthy twist doesn't compromise what we all love about the original, with crispy potato skins, a bunch of crunch, and a cool, sour flavor.

1 Preheat the oven to 400°F (200°C).

2 Place the sweet potatoes on a lined baking sheet and bake for 60 minutes.

3 In a small mixing bowl, combine the cashew cream, apple cider vinegar, lemon juice, garlic, and salt. Set aside in the refrigerator.

4 Remove the potatoes from the oven and let cool so you can handle them easily. Cut each potato lengthwise down the middle. Using a small spoon, scoop out 1 tablespoon of the sweet potato from each skin (see Notes).

5 Place 5 to 7 pepitas in the middle of each skin, then sprinkle nutritional yeast on top. If desired, salt the middle of each skin. Bake in the oven for 15 minutes.

6 Remove from the oven and place a dollop of the cashew cream mixture in the middle of each skin. Sprinkle some green onions and chopped parsley, if using, on top.

7 These are best served immediately, but they will keep in the fridge for at least 4 days.

Makes 10 potato skins

Prep and cook time: 1 hour 30 minutes

5 small sweet potatoes

½ cup (120 ml) Basic Cashew Cream (page 175)

1 tablespoon apple cider vinegar

1 tablespoon lemon juice

1 garlic clove, minced

½ teaspoon salt (or to taste)

2 tablespoons pepitas (pumpkin seeds; see Notes)

2 tablespoons nutritional yeast

⅓ cup (30 g) chopped green onions

2 tablespoons freshly chopped flat-leaf parsley, optional

Notes

* The pepitas are there to add crunch, like the bacon does in the traditional recipe. If you don't have pepitas, you can use sunflower seeds.

* You can use the leftover sweet potato flesh in Sweet Potato Pancakes (page 33).

* If you want to have some garlic sour cream left over for dipping, double the recipe.

HEALTHY COLESLAW

oleslaw is a staple at most family gatherings across America. Some fast-food restaurants serve it, traditional Southern restaurants always seem to have it on the menu, and many families have an old recipe that's passed down from one generation to the next. I find that the problem with most recipes is the mayo—there's lots (and lots) of it. I love a good coleslaw like anyone else, but I cleaned this one up a bit. This recipe literally comes together in just minutes. It also gets better when it's left to sit in the fridge overnight.

1 In a large serving bowl, mix together the shredded carrots and broccoli slaw.

2 In a large liquid measuring cup or a small bowl, add the garlic, tahini, apple cider vinegar, lemon juice, maple syrup, and salt. Whisk well and pour over the slaw. Mix with a spatula until everything is well combined and the slaw is evenly coated.

3 Cover and place in the fridge for 30 minutes for the flavors to blend together a little.

4 Serve or continue to refrigerate for later. This should keep in the fridge for at least a week.

Note

You can use sunflower butter in place of tahini if you prefer, or if you have a sesame allergy.

Makes 6 servings

Prep and chill time: 40 minutes

3 large carrots, shredded

One 12-ounce (340 g) bag broccoli slaw (about 4 cups)

2 garlic cloves, minced

2 tablespoons tahini (see Note)

1½ tablespoons apple cider vinegar

2 teaspoons lemon juice (or the juice of ½ small lemon)

2 teaspoons maple syrup

1 teaspoon salt (or to taste)

ASIAN QUINOA SALAD

This Asian-inspired quinoa salad is packed with vegetables. While the recipes calls for red and yellow peppers, all varieties of peppers work well in this dish. You can also use red onions in place of the green onions if you're looking for a more intense onion flavor. Since the vegetables are all raw, you don't lose any of the health benefits that you normally would during cooking. With that in mind, let the quinoa cool before adding the rest of the ingredients so as not to inadvertently heat the vegetables.

1 In a small saucepan, bring the water and quinoa to a boil. Turn the heat down to medium-low, cover, and let simmer until all the water is absorbed, 10 to 15 minutes. Let the quinoa cool.

2 Once the quinoa has cooled, add it to a large bowl with the remaining salad ingredients. Mix until everything looks well combined.

3 To make the dressing, add all the ingredients to a small bowl. Whisk together.

4 Pour the dressing over the salad and mix well. This should last for at least a week in the fridge.

Notes

* To make things easier, you can prepare the quinoa the day before. This way, it will be completely cooled when you add the rest of the ingredients.

* If you use soy sauce in place of the coconut aminos, make sure to omit the salt. Soy sauce is very salty, so there will be no need for extra salt.

* If you have trouble locating mirin, check the Pantry section on page 12 for a good substitute.

Makes 5 to 6 servings

Prep and cook time: 45 minutes

SALAD

2 cups (480 ml) water

1 cup (170 g) uncooked quinoa (see Notes)

2 cups (180 g) shredded purple cabbage (or ¼ head cabbage, thinly sliced)

1½ cups (235 g) cooked and shelled edamame (or green peas)

2 to 3 green onions, chopped

2 large carrots, shredded

1 red bell pepper, thinly sliced

1 yellow bell pepper, thinly sliced

DRESSING

2 tablespoons coconut aminos (or gluten-free soy sauce; see Notes)

2 tablespoons toasted sesame oil

2 tablespoons mirin (see Notes)

Juice of 1 large lime

½ teaspoon salt (or to taste)

BUCKWHEAT SALAD WITH KALAMATA OLIVES

One of the unique flavor combinations of Mediterranean cuisine is the brine of olives and feta cheese. Greek foods often contain these two ingredients in abundance—we've all had a Greek pasta salad loaded with them. This recipe keeps the same flavor profile but is a healthier version, substituting the carb-heavy pasta with gluten-free buckwheat. The saltiness of the kalamata olives with the fresh touch of the lemon juice really makes this dish. The variety of crisp, raw vegetables adds a nice crunch with each bite, too. This simple dish will be in constant rotation for those who love all things Mediterranean.

1 In a large pot, bring the water to a boil. Add the buckwheat and cook for 15 minutes or until soft.

2 Drain the water from the buckwheat, then run cool water over it to cool it off.

3 Place the cooled buckwheat in a large bowl and stir in the other ingredients. Serve chilled or at room temperature.

Makes 5 to 6 servings

Prep and cook time: 25 minutes

3 cups (720 ml) water

1½ cups (275 g) uncooked buckwheat groats

1 cup (150 g) sliced cherry tomatoes

½ cup (50 g) chopped green onions

½ cup (75 g) diced yellow bell peppers

½ cup (90 g) pitted and chopped kalamata olives

½ medium cucumber, chopped, optional (see Notes)

1 tablespoon lemon juice

2 teaspoons minced roasted garlic (about 5 garlic cloves; see Notes)

1 teaspoon olive oil

1 teaspoon salt (or to taste)

Notes

* The cucumbers are optional depending on how you serve this. If you plan to serve it chilled, the cucumbers are a great addition. If you're serving it at room temperature, I find the cucumbers can get a bit slimy and ruin the dish.

* Fresh flat-leaf parsley would be a great addition. I suggest using ¼ cup (15 g) coarsely chopped parsley.

* The roasted garlic adds a great touch to the whole dish. While you can buy roasted garlic at most grocery stores these days, making your own is easy. Simply cut the top off a bulb of garlic, brush with some oil, wrap it in foil, and place it in the oven for 20 minutes at 350°F (180°C). Once you remove it from the oven, let it cool a bit before removing the garlic from the skins. To mince the garlic, I use a Microplane grater.

THE BEST LEMON ROASTED BROCCOLI

could live on roasted vegetables—I eat them almost every single day. No matter what marinade you use, they always taste perfect. While brussels sprouts are my favorite vegetable to roast, broccoli is a close second—it is simply an amazing plant. One cup of this little tree provides your entire day's worth—and more—of vitamins C and K. (Who says you need sugary orange juice to get your vitamin C?) This recipe is super-simple and turns out wonderfully. You'll want to devour the whole pan! While you're doing that, you can take comfort in eating a food that's considered one of the healthiest for you.

Makes 4 servings

Prep and cook time: 30 to 40 minutes

2 large heads broccoli, cut into florets

2 tablespoons avocado oil (or olive oil)

Juice of 1 small lemon

½ teaspoon garlic powder

½ teaspoon salt (or to taste)

1 Preheat the oven to 350°F (180°C). Line a baking sheet with parchment paper.

2 Toss all the ingredients together in a large mixing bowl, making sure the broccoli is evenly coated.

3 Spread on the baking sheet and bake for 15 minutes.

4 Remove the pan from the oven and shake the broccoli around, then bake for another 10 minutes. The broccoli will still be a little crunchy. If you'd like it to be softer, cook an extra 10 minutes or so.

5 Enjoy! This will last at least a week in the fridge.

Note

Don't discard the broccoli stalks. You can save them to make vegetable broth (see page 16).

STUFFED PEPPERS

Stuffed peppers are always a crowd pleaser. They're simple to make, taste great, and easy to clean up. This recipe calls for just a handful of ingredients, so if you're new to stuffed peppers, this would be a great start. Just be sure the rice is cooked well. The rice at the top of the pepper tends to dry out in the oven, so I like to sprinkle some water on top with my fingers halfway through the baking process, since hard rice is never a good thing.

1 Put all the ingredients except the peppers in a large sauté pan on medium heat. Cook for 10 to 15 minutes. The onions should be soft but not brown. Remove the bay leaf.

2 While the rice mixture is cooking, preheat the oven to 400°F (200°C). This is also a good time to prep the peppers.

3 Cut the tops off the peppers and scoop all the seeds out. Rinse them to get all the seeds out.

4 Stand the peppers in a baking dish, brush the outsides with oil, and fill each pepper with the rice mixture. Bake for about 20 minutes.

5 Serve while they're still warm. They'll keep in the refrigerator for a day or two.

Makes 4 servings

Prep and cook time: 50 minutes

4 cups (760 g) cooked brown rice (see Variations)

⅔ cup (100 g) diced yellow onion

3 garlic cloves, minced

¼ cup (40 g) raisins

2 tablespoons dried parsley

2 tablespoons olive oil

1 bay leaf

1 teaspoon salt (or to taste)

4 red or yellow bell peppers

Variations

- If you prefer, you can use quinoa in place of the rice.

- If you want to spice this up a bit, add ¼ teaspoon ground cumin to the rice mixture as it cooks.

- Chickpeas are a nice protein addition. I recommend using 1 cup (165 g) cooked chickpeas and only 3 cups (570 g) rice.

Notes

- You can make the rice mixture the day before and then cook the peppers right before you serve them.

- When you refrigerate these, they'll soften a bit overnight with all the moisture inside the pepper.

SOUTHWESTERN QUINOA CASSEROLE

eet the Southwestern Quinoa Casserole: vegan comfort food. Quinoa is a plant-based complete protein, so this dish packs a real nutritional punch. It's great for potlucks, parties, and those cold days when you just want something to help warm up. The Macadamia Nut Cheese Sauce makes this dish to die for and adds some great fats to the recipe. You load it all up with tons of fresh veggies and anyone will enjoy this dish.

1 Add the water and quinoa to an ovenproof 9-inch (23 cm) sauté pan (see Notes). Bring to a boil, then turn the heat down to a simmer, cover, and cook until all the water is absorbed, about 10 minutes.

2 Add the green peppers, red peppers, mushrooms, onion, jalapeño, garlic, avocado oil, chili powder, and salt to the pan. Cover and cook for about 7 minutes, stirring often.

3 Preheat the oven to 350°F (180°C).

4 Turn the flame off, add the cheese sauce, tomatoes, black beans, and roasted red peppers, and stir well.

5 Transfer the pan to the lower oven rack and bake for 1 hour.

6 Garnish with cilantro and green onions and serve. This casserole should last at least a week in the fridge.

Notes

- If you don't want this to be spicy, remove the seeds from the jalapeño or just omit it altogether.

- If you don't have an ovenproof pan, cook this in a regular pan and transfer to a 9 × 13 (22 × 33 cm) baking dish.

- This recipe is best served fresh; I don't recommend freezing it.

Makes 5 to 6 servings

Prep and cook time: 1 hour 40 minutes

2 cups (480 ml) water

1 cup (170 g) uncooked quinoa

1 cup (150 g) diced green bell peppers

1 cup (150 g) diced red bell peppers

½ cup (35 g) diced mushrooms

½ cup (80 g) diced yellow onion

1 jalapeño, diced (optional; see Notes)

1 garlic clove, minced

2 tablespoons avocado oil

1 teaspoon chili powder

1 teaspoon salt (or to taste)

2½ cups (600 ml) Macadamia Nut Cheese Sauce (page 171)

2 cups (300 g) chopped cherry tomatoes

1½ cups (255 g) cooked black beans (or one 15-ounce [425 g] can black beans, drained and rinsed)

¼ cup (35 g) chopped roasted red peppers (see page 15)

Chopped cilantro, for garnish

Chopped green onions, for garnish

WHITE BEAN & ZUCCHINI BURGER

Veggie burgers from a box have always let me down. They usually have a rubbery texture and cardboard taste, which is why I prefer homemade veggie burgers. This recipe is super-easy to make with ingredients that won't break the bank, and it allows for so many possibilities. Use a bun or lettuce wrap, or do I as do: Eat them as is, topped with a spread such as Dijon mustard and a side of roasted veggies.

1 Preheat the oven to 350°F (180°C). Line a baking sheet with parchment paper.

2 Add the zucchini and white beans to a food processor and mix for 1 to 2 minutes, until they break down into a coarse texture. You may have to scrape down the sides a few times.

3 Add the diced onion, garlic powder, smoked paprika, and salt and mix for another minute. Next, add the flaxseed meal and the oat flour and mix until everything is incorporated, about 1 minute.

4 Using your hands, form the mixture into small patties and place them on the baking sheet.

5 Bake for 25 to 30 minutes. Let the burgers cool before removing from the baking sheet, about 20 minutes.

6 Serve immediately or refrigerate for later. Store them in an airtight container in the fridge. These should last a couple weeks in the fridge. You can also freeze them for up to 6 months.

Makes 6 small burgers

Prep and cook time: 1 hour

1 small zucchini, chopped

2 cups (360 g) cooked white beans (or one 15-ounce [425 g] can white beans, drained and rinsed)

2 tablespoons diced onion

½ teaspoon garlic powder

½ teaspoon smoked paprika

¼ teaspoon salt (or to taste)

¼ cup (30 g) flaxseed meal

¼ cup (25 g) gluten-free oat flour

SUN-DRIED TOMATO HERB CRACKERS

Crackers are a fantastic snack, even for very young kids. However, if you buy gluten-free vegan crackers at the store, you know how pricey they can get. You can easily make your own at home, where you get to control the ingredients, flavors, and budget. Although this recipe takes a bit of time, it's worth it.

1 Preheat the oven to 350°F (180°C).

2 In a food processor, blend the brown rice and quinoa for 1 minute. Drain the sun-dried tomatoes and add them to the food processor. Blend for another minute. Add the basil, parsley, maple syrup, oregano, and salt. Blend for 30 seconds. Add the water, 1 teaspoon at a time, if the mixture looks dry. You want the mixture to clump together but not be too wet.

3 Tear three sheets of parchment paper the length of one baking sheet. Lay one sheet of parchment paper on the countertop. Take half of the cracker dough and place it in the middle of the parchment paper. Place another sheet of parchment paper on top of that.

4 Using a rolling pin on top of the parchment paper, roll out the mixture until it's about ¼ inch (6 mm) thick (it should cover most of the paper). Transfer the paper with the rolled-out mixture onto a baking sheet. Repeat the same steps with the second half of the dough, placing it on a second baking sheet.

5 Place the baking sheets in the oven and bake for 15 minutes.

6 Pull the baking sheets out of the oven. Using a pizza cutter or knife, cut the dough into squares and then flip each square over.

7 Place the baking sheets back in the oven for another 15 minutes. If the crackers are not crispy at that point, bake them for 5 minutes more.

8 Let the crackers cool completely (about 35 minutes) before storing in an airtight container (see Note). These should last several weeks in the pantry.

Makes 28 to 30 crackers

Prep and cook time: 50 minutes

1½ cups (285 g) cooked brown rice

½ cup (95 g) cooked quinoa

½ cup (25 g) sun-dried tomatoes, soaked in water for 30 minutes

2 teaspoons dried basil

2 teaspoons dried parsley

2 teaspoons maple syrup

½ teaspoon dried oregano

½ teaspoon salt (or to taste)

1 to 2 teaspoons water (if needed)

Note

Store these crackers in an airtight container with rice scattered on the bottom. The rice will absorb moisture and keep them crispy.

SALT & VINEGAR ROASTED CHICKPEAS

Roasted chickpeas are a huge favorite in our house. Both of my girls inhale the sweet version I make, which is nothing short of amazing given their proclamations of hating beans! Roasted chickpeas don't have to be sweet, though. The chickpea has a very distinct but mild flavor that makes it incredibly versatile. The combination of sweet, sour, and salty flavors in these Salt & Vinegar Roasted Chickpeas is out of this world. We never have leftovers—they get scooped up and eaten right off the baking sheet! If you're trying to move away from potato chips, this is a great alternative.

1 In a large bowl, combine the chickpeas, apple cider vinegar, and water. Let the mixture marinate for 3 hours.

2 Preheat the oven to 350°F (180°C). Line a baking sheet with parchment paper or grease it lightly.

3 When the chickpeas are done marinating, drain them in a fine-mesh strainer, then put them back in the bowl they were soaking in.

4 Toss in the avocado oil and salt and mix.

5 Spread the chickpeas on the baking sheet.

6 Bake for 45 minutes, stopping to shake the chickpeas every 10 to 15 minutes.

7 Let the chickpeas cool completely before storing them in an airtight container. These should last for at least 2 weeks in the pantry.

Makes 6 servings

Prep and cook time: 3 hours 50 minutes

3 cups (500 g) cooked chickpeas (or one 25-ounce [708 g] can organic chickpeas, drained and rinsed)

1 cup (240 ml) apple cider vinegar

1 cup (240 ml) water

2 tablespoons avocado oil

2 teaspoons salt (or to taste)

Note

To keep the chickpeas crunchy, scatter some rice at the bottom of the container you store them in. The rice will absorb any excess moisture.

STUFFED MUSHROOMS

This is a super-easy appetizer that party or dinner guests will love. You can make the filling ahead of time and then bake the mushrooms right when the party starts so the dish will be fresh. While most stuffed mushrooms have bread crumbs on top, I decided to use quinoa flakes for that same crunchy effect. This unique twist is my favorite part of the whole recipe; it shows how you can make easy substitutions and not lose what you love about the original.

1 Preheat the oven to 350°F (180°C). Line a baking sheet with parchment paper.

2 Using a damp kitchen towel, clean the tops of the mushrooms. Grab the stems and give them a little twist to remove them from the caps. Set the stems aside and place the caps on the baking sheet.

3 Brush the caps with the olive oil and sprinkle with ½ teaspoon of salt.

4 In a food processor, combine the cashew cream, mushroom stems, onion, parsley, and the remaining salt. Pulse a few times to mix everything up, but not too much (you don't want to completely purée it). Add the quinoa flakes and pulse a few more times.

5 Spoon the stuffing into the caps of each mushroom. I like to pile a little of the stuffing on top, too.

6 When all the mushrooms are stuffed, sprinkle some quinoa flakes and the oregano on top.

7 Bake for about 20 minutes. The tops should be lightly golden brown.

8 Serve immediately for best results, although they can also be stored in the fridge for about 1 week.

Makes 30 stuffed mushrooms

Prep and cook time: 30 minutes

1 pound (450 g) mushrooms (about 30 mushrooms)

2 tablespoons olive oil

1 teaspoon salt

1 cup (240 ml) Basic Cashew Cream (page 175)

½ cup (80 g) diced yellow onion

¼ cup (15 g) freshly chopped flat-leaf parsley

½ cup (50 g) quinoa flakes, plus more for topping (see Variations)

1½ teaspoons dried oregano

Variations

* If you don't have gluten issues, you can use panko bread crumbs instead of quinoa flakes.

* Another twist is to add 2 tablespoons nutritional yeast to the mixture for a cheesy, nutty flavor.

FLOURLESS SNICKERDOODLE BARS

love when I can trick my kids into eating healthy food. While both of them claim to hate beans, they gobble these right up without one complaint. These rich treats come with a hidden ingredient full of protein: the lovable chickpea. I use chickpeas in a variety of ways, including sweet recipes. They're so versatile and provide a texture and moisture similar to dairy-based goods when used in baked goods. It also happens that I love snickerdoodle-flavored anything, so this recipe is a perfect fit for me.

1 Preheat the oven to 350°F (180°C). Line an 8 × 8-inch (20 × 20 cm) baking dish with parchment paper. Make sure you leave some paper sticking out of the sides to make it easier to remove.

2 In a food processor, grind up the chickpeas for 1 minute, then add the oats, almond butter, maple syrup, 1½ teaspoons of the cinnamon, the vanilla extract, baking powder, and salt. Add the flax eggs and blend again until smooth, about 2 minutes.

3 Spoon the mixture into the baking dish. It will be very sticky; using a wet spatula helps.

4 Sprinkle the coconut sugar and the remaining ½ teaspoon cinnamon on top.

5 Bake for 15 minutes, until golden on top.

6 Let it completely cool (about 20 minutes) before removing from the baking pan. Then lift the whole thing out by grabbing the ends of the parchment paper. Use a pizza cutter or knife to cut into bars.

7 Store them in an airtight container in the fridge. They should last about 2 weeks. You can also freeze them for up to 6 months.

Makes 9 large squares or 16 small squares

Prep and cook time: 45 minutes

---

2 cups (330 g) cooked chickpeas (or one 15-ounce [425 g] can chickpeas, drained and rinsed)

1 cup (95 g) gluten-free rolled oats

½ cup (125 g) unsalted almond butter

⅓ cup (80 ml) maple syrup

2 teaspoons ground cinnamon

1 teaspoon vanilla extract

½ teaspoon baking powder

½ teaspoon salt

2 flax eggs (see page 10)

2 tablespoons coconut sugar

PEACH CRUMBLE

The peaches and maple syrup are the perfect combination of sweet and tart in this crumble, and the oats give it that crisp texture. If you want to add a creamy flavor to this dish, some Coconut Whipped Cream (page 181) would go really well with it. This dessert makes the house smell absolutely divine and doesn't last long around my family. Be prepared for everyone to hang over the dish trying to get the last bite.

1 Preheat the oven to 350°F (180°C).

2 Place the sliced peaches in an 8-inch (20 cm) glass pie pan. Sprinkle the flaxseed meal over the peaches and toss with a spatula, then pour 2 tablespoons of the maple syrup over the peaches.

3 In a large mixing bowl, add the oats, the remaining ¼ cup maple syrup, the coconut oil, applesauce, cinnamon, almond extract, and salt. Pour the oat mixture over the peaches.

4 Bake for about 45 minutes. You will see the edges and top turn a slight golden brown once done.

5 Serve immediately. This crumble should last a couple weeks in the fridge.

Makes 6 servings

Prep and cook time: 1 hour

5 peaches, pitted and thinly sliced

1 tablespoon flaxseed meal

¼ cup (60 ml) plus 2 tablespoons maple syrup

1½ cups (145 g) gluten-free rolled oats (see Variations)

3 tablespoons melted coconut oil

2 tablespoons applesauce (see page 7)

2 teaspoons ground cinnamon

1 teaspoon almond extract

½ teaspoon salt

Variations

* This recipe would work great with apples as well.

* For a grain-free version, you can use chopped almonds or pecans in place of the rolled oats.

MIXED BERRY CRISP

My favorite part of holiday meals is dessert, and my favorite desserts are the ones with fruit as the centerpiece. While I love all varieties of fruit, berries really have a special place in my heart. Soft, sugary, and sour-sweet, berries always hit the spot. Filled with strawberries, blackberries, and blueberries, this mixed berry crisp may look fancy but is actually super-easy to make. It would be especially delicious with some creamy vanilla ice cream on top.

1 Preheat the oven to 350°F (180°C).

2 In a large ovenproof sauté pan, add the blackberries, blueberries, strawberries, ¼ cup of the maple syrup, the water, lemon juice, lemon zest, and ½ teaspoon of the salt. Cook on medium heat for 5 to 7 minutes; you want the fruit to still hold its shape but be a little softer.

3 Remove the berries from the heat and add the chia seeds. Stir well and let the mixture stand for about 5 minutes.

4 In a food processor, combine the almond flour, coconut oil, remaining 2 tablespoons maple syrup, ½ teaspoon salt, and the almond extract. Pulse until the mixture starts to come together.

5 Sprinkle the almond flour mixture over the fruit.

6 Place in the oven and bake for about 15 minutes, until golden.

7 Let the crisp cool completely (about 10 minutes) before serving on its own or topped with some Blackberry Ice Cream (page 65) or Coconut Whipped Cream (page 181). This should last about 1 week in the fridge.

Makes 10 to 12 servings

Prep and cook time: 40 minutes

1 pint (about 2 cups [340 g]) blackberries

1 pint (about 2 cups [340 g]) blueberries

2 cups (330 g) sliced strawberries

¼ cup (60 ml) plus 2 tablespoons maple syrup

¼ cup (60 ml) water

Juice of ½ lemon

1 teaspoon grated lemon zest

1 teaspoon salt

2 tablespoons chia seeds

1½ cups (170 g) almond flour (see Notes)

2 tablespoons melted coconut oil (see Notes)

½ to 1 teaspoon almond extract (see Notes)

Notes

* If you have a nut allergy, you can use gluten-free rolled oats in place of the almond flour and vanilla instead of almond extract.

* If you don't use oil, you can use applesauce instead of the coconut oil at the same ratio.

* I add about 1 teaspoon almond extract, but if you prefer a more subtle almond flavor, just add ½ teaspoon.

THREE-INGREDIENT NO-BAKE ALMOND BUTTER COOKIES

My three-ingredient peanut butter cookies, one of my favorite recipes on my blog, were the inspiration for these almond butter cookies. With just three ingredients, they are super-easy to make, and they're even easier to eat. The dates provide a nice caramel flavor, and I can't say enough good things about almond butter. A cousin to peanut butter, almond butter is rich in flavor, protein, and iron. For once, you can feel pretty good about eating cookies.

1 Drain the dates and add them to a food processor with the almond butter and salt. Blend for 1 to 2 minutes, until everything looks well combined. Be careful not to overblend.

2 Line a baking sheet with parchment paper. Using a small cookie scoop, drop the dough onto the baking sheet. Flatten the cookies with a fork, making a crisscross pattern.

3 Place the cookies in the fridge to set up, about 30 minutes.

4 Keep these cookies stored in the fridge. They should last a couple weeks. You can also freeze them for up to 6 months.

Makes 12 cookies

Prep and chill time: 35 minutes

8 Medjool dates, pitted and soaked in water for 30 minutes (see Notes)

1 cup (250 g) unsalted almond butter (see Notes)

½ teaspoon salt

Notes

* If you can't find Medjool dates, you can use another kind of date. You will need to use about 12 total, since Medjool are the largest variety.

* If you have a nut allergy, you can use sunflower butter in place of the almond butter. If you prefer peanut butter, that will also work.

* If you use salted nut butter, skip the salt in the recipe.

MAKE IT YUMMY:
Sauces, Dressings & Other Accompaniments

I f I had known just how easy it is to make my own salad dressing or hummus—or any sauce, dressing, salsa, or spread for that matter—I could have saved a ton of money over the years. Sometimes I think we buy those items from a store just because that's what our family and friends have always done. But it's so easy to make these things yourself! In this section, I'll show you how to start saving money by making some really delicious accompaniments.

HIDDEN VEGGIES TOMATO SAUCE

I don't know about you, but I'm always trying to find a way to get my kids to eat more veggies. It seems that most parents usually accomplish this by sneaking them into dishes. This next recipe is a perfect example of that. Not only does it contain many servings of veggies, but there's also no added sugar. While most tomato sauce recipes call for at least a little sugar, I use carrots and a red pepper to sweeten mine. This freezes well, so you can make a lot when tomatoes are in season and freeze it to enjoy all year long. I make mine in the slow cooker, but you can also make it on the stove (simmering for 2 hours) if you prefer or if time is tight.

1 Place all the ingredients except the arrowroot in a slow cooker and turn on high. Cook for 8 hours.

2 When everything is soft, use an immersion blender to make it smooth.

3 Take a taste and add more seasonings, if necessary. If the sauce looks a bit thin, add 2 to 3 tablespoons arrowroot. Make sure you mix well, as arrowroot tends to clump together.

4 Serve immediately or refrigerate for later. This should last a couple weeks in the fridge and up to 6 months in the freezer.

Makes 6 to 7 cups (1.4 to 1.7 L)

Prep and cook time: 8 hours 30 minutes

15 basil leaves, chopped

12 vine-ripened tomatoes, diced

4 small carrots, peeled and diced

2 to 3 garlic cloves, minced

2 small zucchini, diced (see Notes)

1 red bell pepper, diced

1 yellow onion, diced

1 tablespoon dried parsley (see Notes)

1 teaspoon dried oregano

1 teaspoon salt (or to taste)

½ teaspoon dried thyme

2 to 3 tablespoons arrowroot (if needed)

Notes

- I peeled the zucchini to make sure the color of the sauce didn't change too much. If you prefer, you can keep the skins on.

- If you want to use fresh parsley, I suggest using ¼ cup (15 g), but don't add it until near the end to keep the fresh parsley taste.

- This sauce is great for pasta, pizza, or even as a dipping sauce!

MACADAMIA NUT CHEESE SAUCE

Just because you're vegan doesn't mean you have to give up cheesy-flavored things. If you're new to a vegan or dairy-free diet, or you just want to be a little adventurous, this cheese sauce is a great place to start. Nuts are very versatile and make wonderful vegan cheeses when paired with nutritional yeast. While I use macadamia nuts for this recipe, they can be substituted with cashews and turn out just as well. Both add fat and texture to the sauce, but each nut will impart a slightly different flavor. The macadamia nuts provide richness to this cheese sauce. Once you have this made, you can use it in many different recipes, such as Chili Mac & Cheese, page 85.

1 Drain and rinse the nuts. Add them to a high-power blender with the rest of the ingredients. Blend until smooth.

2 This sauce will last a couple weeks in the fridge. I store mine in a large mason jar. You can also freeze the sauce for up to 3 months.

Makes 3½ cups (600 ml)

Prep time: 5 minutes

2 cups (270 g) raw macadamia nuts, soaked in water overnight (see Note)

2 cups (480 ml) water

1 cup (60 g) nutritional yeast

1 teaspoon salt (or to taste)

½ teaspoon garlic powder

Note

If you forget to soak the nuts overnight, you can boil them for 30 minutes to soften.

LEMON POPPY SEED DRESSING

The secret to most great salad dressing recipes has got to be lemon. It acts as both a preservative in the dressing and adds a refreshing, one-of-kind flavor. I love to create salad dressings that incorporate lemons for that reason. This recipe is a perfect example of that, and it's super-easy to make. After you taste this, you'll never want to buy store-bought dressings again! Plus this is simply more convenient, as there's no driving to a store and standing in line required.

1 Mix all the ingredients in a jar and shake well.

2 Serve immediately or refrigerate for later. Once refrigerated, the dressing may separate and the oil may harden slightly. Just make sure you take it out of the fridge about 30 minutes before you plan to use it. This should last for several weeks in the fridge.

Makes 5 servings

Prep time: 5 minutes

⅓ cup (80 ml) olive oil

Juice of 1 large lemon

2 teaspoons maple syrup

1 garlic clove, minced

1 teaspoon Dijon mustard

1 teaspoon poppy seeds

CREAMY AVOCADO & CILANTRO DRESSING

Salad dressings get made in our house at about the same pace as salads. Both my husband and I try to eat a good amount of green leafy vegetables, and salads are one of those things you can make in advance and eat over a few days. That being said, we're constantly looking for new and delicious ways to dress them. Avocado always makes things better, and this dressing is an homage to that fact. It's a simple recipe and can be whipped up in minutes and made to your taste with a few simple adjustments. A little goes a long way, and it's just another way to enjoy avocado on your salad.

1 Place all the ingredients in a small blender or food processor. Blend until smooth, about 2 minutes.

2 This is best when served immediately, but it will keep in the fridge for about 4 days.

Note

Like all things avocado, browning can be a concern if you're going to store this in the fridge. The acid from the lime helps keep it green with a small amount of browning on top that can be mixed in before serving. You can also pour a little bit of oil on top of the dressing when storing it, to keep the air off it.

Makes 1¼ cup (300 ml)

Prep time: 5 minutes

2 avocados, pitted and peeled

¼ cup (60 ml) water

1 tablespoon lime juice (or the juice of 1 lime)

2 teaspoons freshly chopped cilantro

¼ teaspoon garlic powder

Pinch of salt

TWO-INGREDIENT MAPLE DIJON DRESSING

Makes 4 servings
Prep time: 5 minutes

¼ cup (60 g) Dijon mustard

2 tablespoons maple syrup

Salad dressings are one of the easiest things to make yourself, and this particular homemade version of Dijon dressing is no exception, taking less than 2 minutes to mix together. At home, I make it as I need it; however, you can certainly make a bigger batch by increasing the amounts of Dijon and maple syrup in the same ratio.

1 In a small bowl, whisk together both ingredients. Take a taste and adjust according to your level of sweetness.

2 Serve immediately or refrigerate for later. I like to store mine in 4-ounce (120 ml) mason jars. It should last for at least a few weeks.

Note

If you wanted to brighten up the flavor even more, you could add 1 teaspoon lemon juice.

BASIC CASHEW CREAM

C ashews are so versatile: You can make cheese, cream, sour cream, and salad dressing out of them. They can a bit pricey, though, so it helps to buy them from bulk bins and to buy cashew pieces instead of whole ones. This basic cashew cream recipe allows you to go sweet or savory (see the Variations below for sweet and savory additions). I like to add this to soups, and sometimes I even use it as a frosting. This is an ingredient in some of the other recipes in this book, so it's a good one to try.

Makes 2 cups (240 ml)

Prep time: 5 minutes

1½ cups (210 g) raw cashews, soaked in water overnight

½ cup (120 ml) almond milk

1 Drain and rinse the cashews and add them to a high-power blender with the almond milk. Blend for 3 to 5 minutes. Make sure you stop several times to scrape down the sides. You may need to add a little more milk to reach your desired consistency.

2 Keep this cashew cream in the fridge. I like to store mine in a small mason jar. It should last at least 2 weeks in the fridge.

Variations

* To make a savory cashew cream, add 2 tablespoons apple cider vinegar, 2 tablespoons lemon juice, and a pinch of salt.

* To make a sweet cashew cream, add 2 tablespoons maple syrup and 1 teaspoon ground vanilla beans. This sweet cashew cream can also be put in coffee for a luxurious taste! I suggest adding 1 to 2 teaspoons.

STRAWBERRY SALSA

These days, whether it's at a family gathering or a summer pool party, salsa seems to make an appearance in some form or another. These salsas usually originate from a jar and vary from glorified tomato sauce to something that's so onion-heavy everyone will be standing at least five feet away from you when trying to carry on a conversation. This recipe plays on the sweet and spicy combination that I just love so much. If you want to switch things up a bit at your next gathering or think your salsa-loving family could use an alternative, this strawberry salsa is a must. My husband, who loves all things salsa, devoured this.

Makes 2 cups (480 ml)

Prep and chill time: 35 minutes

2 cups (330 g) diced strawberries

1 jalapeño, seeds removed, diced (see Variations)

2 tablespoons freshly chopped cilantro

1 tablespoon diced red onion

Juice of 1 large lime (or 1½ tablespoons lime juice)

Pinch of salt

1 In a large serving bowl, combine all the ingredients and stir well.

2 Cover and place the bowl in the fridge for 30 minutes for the flavors to marinate.

3 Serve with your favorite protein or with chips. This should last 3 to 4 days in the fridge.

Variations

* If you like things extra-spicy, feel free to leave the seeds in the jalapeño.

* This recipe would also be delicious if you added about ½ cup (85 g) diced mango or diced pineapple.

RASPBERRY VANILLA CHIA JAM

My kids love to add jam to their toast in the morning, but most store-bought jams are loaded with unnecessary ingredients and processed sugars. To make matters worse, a lot of homemade jams require canning. This can be quite the daunting process with two little ones running around, trying to get "just a taste" at every turn. This easy jam recipe requires no canning, pectin, or refined sugars and can be made in just minutes. The chia gives it an extra-healthy twist, adding omega-3 fatty acids, fiber, and a bit of protein to the mix. It's also what holds it all together, as the chia becomes a bit sticky. Once you learn how chia acts when it gets wet, the limits are endless in its applications.

1 Blend the raspberries in a food processor. Add the remaining ingredients and blend for another minute.

2 Transfer the mixture to a 16-ounce mason jar and place it in the fridge. It should take about 30 minutes to set up. This should keep in the fridge for several weeks. You can also freeze it for up to 6 months.

Makes 2 cups (480 ml)

Prep and chill time: 30 minutes

3 cups (375 g) fresh raspberries (or frozen and thawed) (see Variations)

3 to 4 tablespoons chia seeds

2 tablespoons maple syrup

1 teaspoon ground vanilla beans (see Variations)

Variations

• This recipe works with any berry, so feel free to experiment. I think a mix of blackberries and raspberries would be delicious as well.

• You can use vanilla extract in place of the ground vanilla beans. If you use extract, reduce the amount to ½ teaspoon.

Note

This jam is very versatile. Not only do I use it in my Chocolate Raspberry Brownies (page 126), but it also makes a great filling for bars and is a lovely topping for pancakes (page 33).

COCONUT WHIPPED CREAM

Just because you're a vegan doesn't mean you have to miss out on whipped topping! You can make this in just a few minutes. Thick, creamy, and luxurious, you won't even want to remember what the dairy variety tastes like. This makes a great topping for puddings and ice creams, a wonderful cake frosting and mousse, or even a dip for a cookie. The uses are endless and the recipe simple.

Makes about 2 cups (475 ml)

Prep time: 5 minutes

One 13.5-ounce can (400 ml) full-fat coconut milk, refrigerated overnight (see Notes)

2 tablespoons maple syrup

1 teaspoon ground vanilla beans

1 Open the can of coconut milk. You will see a solid white layer on top. This is the coconut cream. Scoop that off and put it in the bowl of a stand mixer.

2 Add the maple syrup and vanilla beans to the mixing bowl.

3 Using a whipping attachment, whip the coconut cream for several minutes. Start at a slow speed and then gradually increase until you are on the highest setting. It should take 4 to 5 minutes of whipping to make the whipped cream.

4 Use immediately. This is best when fresh, since it will harden slightly in the fridge.

Variation

If you want to make a chocolate frosting from this cream, just add about ¼ cup (25 g) cocoa powder with the rest of the ingredients.

Notes

* You must have full-fat coconut milk for this recipe to work. I have the best results with Thai Kitchen Organic.

* There will be some coconut water left over in the can of coconut milk. You can freeze that in ice cube trays and use it to add flavor to smoothies.

* If you want to add creaminess to savory dishes, you can make this cream plain; just omit the vanilla beans and maple syrup. Plain coconut cream is a wonderful addition to soups.

SALTED CARAMEL SAUCE

alted caramel seems to be everywhere these days. I used to think it was off-limits for vegans, but I found a way to make an amazing salted caramel sauce that works. As a bonus, it has only three ingredients and is healthier than traditional caramel. This sauce is great for smoothies, desserts, ice cream, cookies, and even oatmeal (I use it in the overnight oats recipe on page 136). The possibilities are endless—you're limited only by your imagination. Even though this is made with coconut milk and coconut sugar, you can't taste the coconut—all you'll taste is caramel goodness.

Makes 1 cup (240 ml)

Prep and cook time: 40 minutes

One 13.5-ounce (400 ml) can full-fat coconut milk (see Note)

¼ cup (50 g) coconut sugar

1 teaspoon salt

1 In a small saucepan, combine the coconut milk and coconut sugar. If the coconut milk has separated in the can, use a spoon to mix it back together.

2 Cook on medium heat for about 10 minutes. Watch it carefully, because the milk may bubble over.

3 As the mixture reduces, turn down the heat periodically. It should take 25 to 30 minutes to reduce down to a caramel-like consistency.

4 Once it looks like caramel, stir in the salt and remove from the heat.

5 Allow it to cool in the pan, then transfer to a glass jar. This should last up to 2 weeks in the fridge.

Note

It's important to make sure you use full-fat canned coconut milk for this recipe.

PICK-ME-UPS:
Juices & Smoothies

can't stress enough how important hydration is. Headaches, stomach pain, soreness, and other ailments can all be traced back to a lack of proper hydration. While I drink mostly water, my family and I occasionally enjoy other drinks and smoothies as meal replacements or supplements. I also use juices as a way to boost my family's immune system during flu season and when school starts back up. Drinks shouldn't be empty calories like they are in sodas. The drink recipes in this chapter have targeted health benefits and aim to keep your taste buds happy at the same time.

ENERGIZING GREEN JUICE

Juicing is a great way to get your vegetables in without feeling overwhelmed. While the topic of juicing can fill entire books, I'll give you the highlights here. First, it's best to drink fresh juice within 24 hours of making it. Second, the best time to drink juice is in the morning, on an empty stomach. Third, after you drink your morning juice, wait 30 minutes before consuming anything else. These are the three simple rules I follow when I juice. This recipe is one I've been making for a long time, and it's meant to be an easy starter to the world of juicing. The flavor is not too sweet and not too bitter—it's mild with a hint of sweetness from the apple.

1 Juice all the ingredients in the order they're listed.

2 For best results, serve immediately. You can store the juice in the fridge for up to 24 hours, but any longer than that and the enzymes will be lost.

Notes

- If you don't have a juicer, you can purée everything in a blender and then pass through a fine-mesh strainer.

- If you like a sweeter juice, you can always add a second apple.

Makes 4 servings

Prep time: 5 minutes

10 kale leaves

1 large cucumber

4 celery stalks

1 apple, cored (see Notes)

1 lemon, peeled

JUICES & SMOOTHIES

185

BEET, ORANGE & GINGER JUICE

Beet juice has many benefits. It works to cleanse the blood and protects against some forms of cancer, colon cancer in particular. Beet juice is high in many vitamins and minerals, such as potassium, folate, fiber, vitamin C, and magnesium. Beets can have an earthy taste, but I find that peeling them helps reduce it. The orange and ginger complement the sweetness of the beets and mask some of those earthy tones. Since the beets make this juice so vibrant in color, it's easier to hide greens in it for the kids. See page 185 for more juicing basics.

1 Using a juicer, juice all the ingredients in the order they're listed.

2 This is best when served fresh but will keep for 12 hours in the fridge.

Makes 4 servings

Prep time: 15 minutes

2 medium oranges, peeled and chopped (see Variation)

2 carrots, trimmed and roughly chopped

2 Swiss chard leaves

1 medium beet, trimmed, peeled, and chopped

½-inch (1.25 cm) piece ginger, peeled

Variation

If you prefer, you can use apples in place of the oranges.

Note

If you don't have a juicer, you can use a high-power blender and then pass it through a fine-mesh strainer.

FRUITY LEMONADE

I love lemons. I put them in my water when I work out, as they're known to help replenish electrolytes. I use them in lots of my recipes, since they freshen up everything they touch. In this lemonade, they provide that sour flavor I love. The honeydew melon adds sweetness, but it also adds its own health benefits. It's high in vitamins C and B6, and in potassium, making it a great fruit to consume if you think you're getting a cold.

1 Juice all the ingredients except the maple syrup. Take a taste, and if you want it to be sweeter, add the maple syrup.

2 Serve immediately or refrigerate for later. This should last up to 4 days in the fridge. You can also freeze it in ice cube trays to add to smoothies in the future.

Makes 4 servings

Prep time: 15 minutes

4 to 5 cups (680 to 850 g) cubed honeydew melon

3 mangoes, pitted and peeled

2 lemons, peeled (see Notes)

1 to 3 teaspoons maple syrup, optional

Notes

* If you like your lemonade a bit less sour, use one lemon instead of two.

* You can make this in a blender if you don't have a juicer. Just blend up the honeydew and mangoes in a high-power blender. Juice the lemons separately and then add to the blender. Blend until smooth.

ALMOND JOY SMOOTHIE

I wish I could take credit for discovering that creamy chocolate and coconut with a hint of almond flavoring are a trio of flavors that seemingly never gets old. Nevertheless, I do know how to re-create it. This smoothie not only tastes like a dessert, it also provides a good amount of protein with the rolled oats and almond butter. The coconut milk provides some fats, and the bananas add some sweetness. Voilà, you have a healthy smoothie for all ages!

1 In a high-power blender, combine all the ingredients except the chocolate chips and blend until smooth. This takes only a minute or two.

2 Pour and garnish with the chocolate chips, if using. Serve immediately or freeze in ice cube trays for reblending later.

Makes 2 servings

Prep time: 5 minutes

2 frozen bananas

1½ cups (360 ml) coconut milk (or one 13.5-ounce [400 ml] can coconut milk)

¼ cup (25 g) gluten-free rolled oats (or quinoa flakes)

2 tablespoons unsalted almond butter (see Variations)

1½ tablespoons cacao powder

½ teaspoon almond extract

Handful of chocolate chips for garnish, optional

Variations

* If you have a nut allergy, you can use sunflower butter instead of almond butter.

* If you want to add some greens like spinach or kale to this, I suggest using ½ cup (8 g) loosely packed greens. Add the greens and the milk to the blender first and blend them together for at least 1 minute before adding the remaining ingredients.

TROPICAL GREEN SMOOTHIE

A whole food vegan cookbook wouldn't be complete without a green smoothie recipe. Unlike 90 percent of smoothie recipes out there, this one contains no bananas and instead uses pineapple as a base. Since I prefer to use real food protein sources over protein powders, I added some hemp seeds and chia seeds. The hemp hearts are also a great source of omega-3 fatty acids. With the healthy fat and protein in this recipe, this smoothie should keep you full until lunchtime. Plus it doesn't hurt that it's tasty.

1 In a high-power blender, add the spinach, almond milk, hemp hearts, and chia seeds. Blend for about 1 minute, or until all the spinach has been blended up.

2 Add the remaining ingredients and blend for 1 to 2 minutes until fully combined.

3 Serve immediately with a sprinkling of hemp and chia seeds, if desired.

Note

If you want to make this ahead of time, you can blend everything and pour into ice cube trays. Then in the morning, just pop out what you need and blend again before serving.

Makes 2 servings

Prep time: 15 minutes

2 cups (40 g) loosely packed spinach or kale

½ cup (120 ml) almond milk

2 tablespoons hemp hearts, plus more for optional topping

1 tablespoon chia seeds, plus more for optional topping

2 cups (340 g) chopped honeydew melon

2 cups (260 g) crushed ice

2 cups (330 g) pineapple chunks

STRAWBERRY MANGO SMOOTHIE

Strawberries are more than a good treat—they're high in B vitamins and vitamin C. B vitamins help you maintain beautiful hair and nails, and have even been linked to reducing the chance of stroke. Vitamin C is good for the immune system. Mango has health benefits for the eyes, hair, and nails as well. It's also considered one of the most consumed fruits in the world. Together, the two make for a wonderfully healthy smoothie.

1 Put all the ingredients in a high-power blender and blend until smooth, 2 to 3 minutes.

2 For best results, serve immediately, sprinkled with chia seeds, if desired.

Makes 4 servings
Prep time: 5 minutes

2 mangoes, peeled and pitted

8 ounces (225 g) strawberries (about 8 large strawberries)

1 cup (240 ml) coconut water

1 cup (130 g) crushed ice

1 tablespoon chia seeds, plus more for optional topping

Note

If you want to make things easier on yourself in the morning, you can prep all the fruits the night before. Then all you need to do is blend.

PEACH RASPBERRY SMOOTHIE

My family loves peach season—our only complaint is that it doesn't last longer. This fruit is beloved around the world, and just one bite will tell you why. Peaches have many health benefits, too. They help reduce stress, contain nutrients that assist in cleansing the liver and kidneys, can aid in ailments such as gout, are high in antioxidants and fiber, are low in calories, and the list goes on and on. The coconut water aids in replenishing your electrolytes, so this a great low-calorie post-workout smoothie.

1 Put all ingredients in a blender and blend until smooth.

2 Serve immediately or pour into ice cube trays and freeze for later. When you want a smoothie, just pop out a few frozen cubes and blend.

Makes 4 servings

Prep time: 5 minutes

2 peaches, pitted

2 cups (250 g) fresh raspberries (thawed frozen berries will work, too)

1 cup (240 ml) coconut water

1 cup (130 g) crushed ice

1 teaspoon ground vanilla beans

BLUEBERRY MUFFIN SMOOTHIE

Blueberries are one superfood you shouldn't do without. They're extremely high in antioxidants, and you get the most benefit from their healthy profile when you consume them raw. The banana serves as a sweetener in this recipe, but with its high potassium levels it also adds to the health aspect of this recipe. The best part is that you'll feel as if you're drinking a blueberry muffin. It tastes like one without all the added sweeteners and preservatives, making this a "blueberry muffin" you can feel good about.

1 Place all the ingredients in a blender and blend until smooth, 1 to 3 minutes.

2 Serve immediately or freeze in ice cube trays for later.

Makes 3 servings

Prep time: 5 minutes

1 frozen banana

1½ cups (225 g) fresh or frozen blueberries

1 cup (240 ml) almond milk

¼ cup (25 g) gluten-free rolled oats (see Variation)

1 tablespoon chia seeds

Variation

If you don't want to use oats, you can replace them with quinoa flakes.

CHERRY CHOCOLATE SMOOTHIE

This is a fun dessert smoothie that's meant more as a treat than anything. The cherries and chocolate are a great combination. The chocolate chips and cacao powder make this smoothie decadently rich. If you think you need a sweeter taste, the Medjool dates will add that bit of sweetness you and your family crave. If it's too rich, you can cut back on the chocolate just a bit and increase the almond milk to get the flavor you're looking for.

1 Put all the ingredients in a blender and blend until smooth.

2 Serve immediately for best results.

Makes 3 or 4 servings

Prep time: 5 minutes

3 cups (465 g) frozen sweet cherries

1¼ cups (300 ml) almond milk

½ cup (90 g) chocolate chips

¼ cup (25 g) cacao powder

2 Medjool dates, pitted, optional, if you desire a sweeter taste

SUNSHINE SMOOTHIE

Nothing says summer like watermelon and cantaloupe. My baby girl, Olive, loves both of those fruits, so I made this smoothie with her in mind. It's like a burst of sunshine in your mouth, with the orange of the cantaloupe and the red of the watermelon mixing together to make a beautiful smoothie. This would be a great vessel to add some veggies as well.

1 Place all the ingredients in a high-power blender and blend for 2 to 3 minutes.

2 For best results, drink immediately. You can also pour this into ice cube trays and freeze for later; then all you need to do is pop out a few frozen cubes and blend.

Makes 4 servings
Prep time: 5 minutes

2 cups (260 g) crushed ice

2 cups (320 g) cubed very ripe cantaloupe

2 cups (300 g) cubed very ripe seedless watermelon

Juice of 1 large lime

Variations

* Some veggies that would hide well in this are carrots or sweet potatoes. Add ½ cup (65 g) chopped of either.

* You can make this into ice pops for a frozen treat. Just blend, pour into molds, and freeze for 6 hours.

* If you want to include some protein, you can add 2 tablespoons chia seeds or hemp hearts.

* Gluten-free rolled oats may be another great addition. I suggest using ¼ cup (25 g) of gluten-free rolled oats.

Note

For best results, make sure you use ultra-ripe melons.

Acknowledgments

First and foremost, I would like to thank my readers. Without you, none of this would be possible. Thank you for your loyalty and for testing all these recipes. Your feedback is appreciated. Also, I would like to thank all the talented people who helped put this book together. Thank you to my publisher, Matthew Lore; my editor, Allie Bochicchio, for helping me every step of the way; the managing editor, Jeanne Tao; the production manager, Pamela Schechter; the art director, Sarah Smith, and the design and production associate, Sarah Schneider, for making this book beautiful inside and out; my publicity and marketing manager, Jennifer Hergenroeder; and the publicity assistant, Vivienne Woodward. Lastly, thank you to anyone who has ever made any of my recipes.

Index

Note: Page references in *italics* indicate recipe photographs.

EASY. WHOLE. VEGAN.

About the Author

MELISSA KING is the writer, photographer, and recipe developer for the popular blog *My Whole Food Life*. A vegetarian for 16 years, in 2012 she went vegan and quit processed foods with her family. Her recipes have been featured on the *Today* show, the *Huffington Post*, *Shape* magazine, *Fitness* magazine, PopSugar Moms, Buzzfeed, and *Everyday Health*. She is also the author of *DIY Nut Milks, Nut Butters & More*. She lives in Dallas, Texas, with her husband and two daughters.